Woodturning
A Fresh Approach

For Cheryl, Kiri and Chloe who provide me with light on dark days, and for my parents who taught me the value of creativity at an early age.

Acknowledgements

I shall be forever grateful to my father John Chapman, and my good friend Mike Pursey, both of whom gave up many days to help with the workshop photography. It is their guidance, critique and patience that have helped make the instructional chapters so clear.

A special thankyou to my wife Cheryl, who has provided much needed guidance and support during the writing of the book, and also for providing the initial inspiration to write it in the first place.

My thanks to David Ellsworth for sharing his wisdom and writing the foreword to this book. Also for providing me with the inspiration to pursue the art of hollow turning.

For helping with Chapter 2, I would like to thank Andy Ball and Charlie Overton-Fox who shared their valuable knowledge and experience of tree felling and allowed me to photograph them at work. Thanks also to Dave Bates (of Stiles & Bates) for sharing his knowledge on timber conversion, and to Bob Smith (of Timberline) for his knowledge of exotic timber species.

Thanks also to Patricia Kenyon for her kind permission in allowing me to use *The Walnut Root Bowl*, to Phil Harding and Bill Jones for their advice on historical details, to Trevor Dawes, Melvyn Firmager, John Hunnex, Bert Marsh, Terry Murphy, Dave Regester and Keith Rowley for their advice early on in the book's infancy, and to Axminster Power Tools, Brimarc, Chris Stott, GPS Agencies and Robert Sorby Tools for their co-operation.

Finally, to all my friends and fellow craftsmen who have helped by providing inspiration and information over the years. And to all those around the world who continue to pass on information for the benefit of us all.

Woodturning
A Fresh Approach

Robert Chapman

Foreword by David Ellsworth

GUILD OF MASTER CRAFTSMAN PUBLICATIONS LTD

First published 1999 by
Guild of Master Craftsman Publications Ltd,
166 High Street, Lewes,
East Sussex, BN7 1XU

All photographs by Robert Chapman except;
John Chapman: Figs 2.24, 2.26, 3.6, 3.9, 3.11, 3.12, 4.1–4.24,
9.7–9.10, 10.1–10.9, 10.11–10.23, 11.1–11.4, 11.6–11.10, 12.3–12.18,
14.3, 14.4, 15.1–15.12, 19.12–19.14, 19.16
Mike Pursey: Figs 2.18, 2.19, 3.7, 3.8, 5.1–5.12, 5.14, 5.15, 6.1–6.12,
7.1–7.9, 8.3–8.6, 8.8–8.18, 11.11–11.14, 13.3, 13.6, 13.9, 14.1, 14.2,
14.5, 16.2–16.13, 17.1, 17.2, 17.4–17.9, 17.12, 17.14–17.17,
18.1–18.3, 18.5, 18.6, 19.5–19.11, 19.15
Illustrations by Robert Chapman, redrawn by John Yates

The publishers and author can accept no legal responsibility for any
consequences arising from the application of information, advice or
instructions given in this publication.

ISBN 1 86108 119 7
A catalogue record of this book is available from the British Library

Designed by Ian Hunt Design
Cover design by Wheelhouse Design
Typeface: Goudy and Trade Gothic

Colour origination by Viscan Graphics (Singapore)
Printed in Great Britain at the University Press, Cambridge

Contents

Foreword

I
T IS A VERY GOOD TIME to be a woodturner! From the humble turning workshops that Albert Le Coff began in Philadelphia in 1976, we now have dozens of local, regional and national seminars and conferences held every year throughout the world. Ten national woodturning organizations are helping to sustain international interest and communication, the largest being the American Association of Woodturners, with over 7,000 members and 125 chapters. The plethora of books, videos, tools and teaching opportunities available today are enough to bring the weary out of retirement and cause our kids to question the value of 'traditional' career goals. And we now have a new organization in America – the Collectors of Wood Art (CWA) – whose sole purpose is to seek out, learn from and acquire woodturnings.

The traditions of making functional ware in woodturning came primarily from our roots in industry over the past century. These traditions began to change during the early 1970s through the efforts of a small number of individuals, most of whom received their education in the fine arts. Largely inspired by the Modern Movement of Craft that emerged out of the 1960s, they began to explore the lathe as a tool for making non-utilitarian 'decorative objects'. These efforts resulted in natural-edged bowls, hollow vessels and pots, totems, sculpture, furniture, and architectural and environmental installations.

With these objects we began to see an approach to the process of making that focused on a very distinct and personalized language of both form and style. Instead of multiples of the same design, each object was conceived and executed as an individual statement and, as such, each became a direct reflection of its maker. Many of these forms drew their visual strength from surface manipulations and enhancements that sometimes included the use of distressed or decomposed materials, texturing with fire or chisel or chainsaw and – horror of horrors – some were even painted! The common denominator among all these people's works was their excellence in craftsmanship and strong emphasis on good design! The result is that by 1982, we had established the foundational roots of the design styles and motifs that we see in all decorative objects being produced in woodturning today.

One result of this shift from functional ware to decorative objects is that by the mid-1980s, turned wood began to gain acceptance from the more established craft media fields, such as ceramics, glass and jewelry. And with this recognition, turners began the long struggle of achieving legitimacy for their work as a viable 'art form'

within the Modern Movement of Craft. Secondly, but no less in importance, is that this 'new' work helped to cultivate a marketplace for turned wood that would compete directly with objects in all craft media. Prior to this period there were *buyers*; now there were *collectors*. So, as the 'craft' of woodturning began to develop an 'art' consciousness, one can appreciate how the prices of these objects have subsequently elevated from the tens to the hundreds and, in some cases, into the thousands of dollars. One must also consider that beyond the strength of the works themselves, the struggle for recognition was somewhat eased as woodturners walked into exhibition venues and a marketplace that was already established by the other craft media fields. And while we have benefitted greatly from their experiences, it is also clear that we have inherited some of their baggage; namely, the craft/art conundrum.

The road from craft to art is a slippery one indeed. There are no maps, accurate guidelines or distance markers. The direction one takes is less relevant than the direction one has taken. There are no rules that can't be broken or formulae that can't be changed. And once you feel you have arrived, you're likely to discover that you've just begun . . . or maybe you were there all the time. Thus, to pursue art as a 'thing' – which seems to be endemic within the traditions of craft – is to ignore the importance of the 'journey'. What seems important then, is to accept the value of the creative process that exists within each of us, and to be very careful not to diminish the importance of Craft in favour of the temptations of Art.

Today, we have begun to chisel away at the traditional academic 'rules' that have defined craft and art for centuries. For the most part, this 'shift' has occurred because the extraordinary work produced within the crafted arts in all media demanded recognition. It is, of course, an ongoing process that carries its own rewards and responsibilities. It is also a challenging time for us all, for the field has never been more open or receptive to good work – regardless of the type of objects we make or each maker's intent. And this is why it is an especially good time to be a woodturner.

Robert Chapman is among a growing number of very talented individuals who have gravitated to woodturning over the past few decades and become full-time studio craftspersons. His working methods and the objects shown here represent a culmination of his passion for making, and the many influences that have inspired him. The reader thus becomes the beneficiary of his efforts, for no-one can predict what influence Chapman's work might have upon us.

DAVID ELLSWORTH

Introduction

WOOD IS ONE OF THE WORLD'S most precious resources and I have always had a deep fascination for the timber I use in my work. Each and every piece was once part of a living sculpture, generously giving its oxygen and painting the landscape with colour through the seasons. As a woodturner I feel privileged to work with such a valuable material – valuable to the wellbeing of our planet and to us all.

When using such a fine material as wood we are duty bound to make the best work we can from it. It may have been felled from a managed forest as part of a crop, removed as part of a development scheme or even blown down in a gale. Whatever the source, this book will provide you with a greater understanding of the characteristics of wood, and the techniques necessary to turn it into attractive and tactile designs. The wood will then be given a new life as a lasting tribute to the tree whence it came.

This book is aimed at readers with a basic knowledge of turning principles (such as those described in any of the foundation course books available). Its purpose is to enable all woodturners, from intermediate to advanced, to realize their full potential. While the text gives detailed step-by-step instructions, more experienced woodturners will find most of the information they need in the illustrations.

The projects, or creative learning exercises as I prefer to call them, are grouped in three sections. They have been selected in order to cover the widest possible range of woodturning techniques and to allow you to build and hone your skills. The exercises are not intended to be followed religiously; they should be adapted to suit your ability and personal preference. Tailor each one so that it is challenging enough to improve your skill, but not so advanced that it is no longer enjoyable. Woodturning should be fun, not a chore. As you learn more techniques and are able to create more varied designs, the more enjoyment you will have.

If you are at all wary of any of the exercises, sit back and look at each one in stages. By breaking them down you will see that they all share common characteristics. There are only three basic forms of line: flat or straight lines, convex lines and concave lines. There are also only three basic movements you can perform with a tool: push and pull, lift and lower, arc and rotate. If you are asked to do any of these in isolation you will probably have no trouble, but it is the combination of skills and movements that enables us to create. If you isolate each basic method, and practise with different tools, you will soon find you are well on the way to greater things.

Early ceramic vessels were purely functional, created to hold foodstuffs and liquids. But it was not long before the

Spalted ash. Diameter: 4½in (114mm).
Wood is anything but predictable. It is this unpredictability that makes timber such an attractive medium to work with.

bowls became decorated, and the shapes more graceful. As woodturners you also have the opportunity to create beautifully made bowls. An aesthetic appreciation of form is within us all, it just needs to be released.

While a few of the designs in this book are functional, most were created for their aesthetic appeal rather than for what they might, or might not hold. Some may appear similar to what has been done in the past, others more original. When you look at the design of a fellow craftsman, beware before you rush in and say 'that's a copy of a Joe Bloggs ceramic pot'. Instead, ask yourself where Joe Bloggs got the idea. The chances are, their sources of inspiration have the same ancient origins. Imagine the creative process as a large communal cooking pot to which each generation adds ingredients and from which each of us is permitted to draw. If we did not pass on information or learn from others we would not advance. However, if I have included designs that any craftsman believes to be of their sole creation, this is purely unintentional and I apologize unreservedly.

Perfect form

I often come across woodturners and potters who talk about their quest for the ever elusive perfect form. While not wishing to offend any of the afore-mentioned, I do not subscribe to this way of thinking. I believe that perfect form is that which harmonizes with the materials used, which conveys a good sense of proportion, and which does the job it was designed to do. Perfect form must be held in context with the requirements of the finished piece. A functional bowl intended for displaying fruit on a low coffee table will need to be stable and have a large base, it could also be quite shallow. A vessel that is to be sited on a high shelf would look lost with such a shape, so it would not be the perfect form for this purpose, regardless of how graceful the profile was. In this case, a much narrower and taller design may be more suited.

I prefer to think of purity of form rather than perfect form – a graceful, flowing line, uninterrupted and free from any sudden changes in curvature. Perfect form to me means creating exactly what I set out to achieve without compromise, when I can see no way of improving the end result, even when viewed from all angles. This said, such pieces are not common. I hope that the information in this book will not only help improve your technical ability, but also your aesthetic appreciation. Soon you will be several steps nearer to achieving your own perfect forms.

Most of us turn for enjoyment. As a professional I still get great satisfaction from turning, perhaps more so than when I began. At first this enjoyment is often given a boost by someone congratulating you on your talent. Later it comes largely from the creation itself. I hope that once you have made a few of the examples in the book, compliments for your work are many.

Before leaving you to enjoy the rest of the book, I would like to share with you a compliment paid to me some years ago – a poem inspired by a bowl I made from a walnut tree that was blown down in the 1987 hurricane. (This hurricane hit southern England in October 1987, causing severe and widespread damage, with a great loss of trees.)

The Walnut Root Bowl

Patricia Kenyon

A Walnut tree
     Free standing,
Peaceful in this Kentish village.
Beaten yearly; felt her fruit landing;
A ritual, not meant as a pillage.
Seeing the seasons' fast passage,
Part of the life of the people,
Repeating the flower, fruit and fall.

     Then came the shock of The Storm.

A Walnut tree
     Now lying,
Peaceful in this Kentish village.
Beaten sorely – felt her trunk landing
Not a ritual – this was a carnage!
Ending all seasons and passage
Knowing the grief of the people.
The wind took the trees from them all.

     Then came the man with his saw.

The Walnut root
     Now turning.
Exited at journeying further.
Lathed tenderly – now they pay homage,
Not a ritual – this is adventure.
Creating, designing such beauty
Seeing the joy of the people;
For wood gives a primitive call.

     The gift of a woodturner's skill.

Safety

A S THIS BOOK IS AIMED AT READERS with some woodturning experience, I have assumed that you will also have a basic knowledge of safety considerations, although all of us would benefit from a reminder now and then so as not to become too complacent. For this reason, some aspects of safety are mentioned throughout the book as and when they are relevant. The following supplementary list by no means covers everything, nor is it in any specific order. Remember the biggest guard against accidents is to think first and use your common sense.

● Avoid working when you are tired. Many aspects of woodturning require total concentration and alertness, especially when you are learning new techniques.
● Keep the work area clean and tidy. Trailing cables and heaps of tools can lead to accidents. Always put tools and polishes away in a safe place. If there are children about, lock the workshop.
● Maintain your equipment. Blunt tools require force which leads to a loss of control. Machinery should be regularly inspected for signs of wear and any faults should be rectified immediately. Always read the owner's manuals.
● Check that the work is properly secured in the lathe and rotate it by hand to ensure that it is clear of the tool rest before starting the lathe. Never leave work in a chuck overnight without tightening it again the next day. This is particularly important when working part-seasoned wood as shrinkage of the wood will cause a loss of grip.
● Always use the correct speed. If you are turning large pieces or work that has an irregular shape, check that you have selected a low speed first and stand to one side, out of the firing line, when you first switch on.

● Make sure you can stop the lathe in an emergency. Is your stop button in easy reach at all times without you having to cross the path of the revolving wood? If not, have a separate, movable switch fitted.
● Eye protection is essential when using any form of machinery or compressed air. A face shield is better still. If you wear glasses, ensure they are shatterproof and wear fitted side shields; if not use over-goggles. For all hollow turning and natural edge work, full face protection is necessary.
● Wear sensible clothing. Avoid loose sleeves and sandals, and keep long hair tied back.
● Protect against dust inhalation. At the least, always wear a mask, but better still use a powered respirator. Some form of dust extraction is also advisable, even more so when power sanding. Beware when sanding fine details by hand as the spinning edges may be razor sharp. Remove the tool rest when sanding to avoid your hand becoming trapped between the rest and the moving work.
● Always switch off machinery when making adjustments. This applies just as much whether you need to move the tool rest on the lathe or lower the guard on the bandsaw.
● Always check your material. Wood is unpredictable, and will often contain bark pockets, large or small cracks and so on. If you are in any doubt as to the stability of the wood, discard it.
● When felling trees always work in pairs whether you are using an axe, bowsaw or chainsaw. Whenever you use a chainsaw, make sure you are wearing the full protective outfit and have had the correct training.
● Do not take risks. Know your limits. If you are not sure of your ability to undertake a task safely, wait until you are more experienced or avoid it altogether.

PART ONE

First Steps

1

workshop and
CONTENTS

THE WORKSHOP AND ITS CONTENTS are the very heart of the woodturning environment. For many woodturners the space occupied is just a small area within a garden shed or at one end of a garage. However, as a passion for turning grows and new equipment is purchased, such a small space is no longer adequate. The garden tools, lawnmower and car will be evicted and new shelves and cupboards fixed to any remaining area of wall space until there is no more room left.

For many, this is a familiar story, and it is the gradual process of laying out a workshop around existing equipment that causes the biggest problems. First comes the lathe and bench grinder. You hurriedly fix them at one end of the workshop believing that you won't be using them often and therefore, they don't require a lot of space. But suddenly you find you are hooked on the woodturning bug and you buy a bandsaw to cut your own wood. There is no room left near the lathe so you position the bandsaw at the other end of the workshop. You know you ought to move that lathe to a better spot, but feel it would take too long. Then comes extra timber. You would like it stored near the bandsaw, but there is no storage space left there . . . Before you know it you have filled all your available space, and nothing is where you would most like it to be.

Layout

As this book is aimed at those who already have some woodturning experience, I shall assume that you already have some sort of workshop area. If not, or you are planning a new one, take a little time to plan where things will go and, if possible, leave room for any later expansion. Draw a plan of the workshop and use scaled cut-outs of the main equipment to find how you can use the space to your best advantage. If there is natural light coming into the workshop, try and use this as much as you can, although you will still need additional illumination for the work area. This is best provided

using a combination of spot lights and angle poise lights: fluorescent lights on their own can cause a stroboscopic effect on the rotating work.

Try and keep the bench grinder and bandsaw close to the lathe as these will be used most frequently. If they are positioned too far away, it is tempting not to use them enough; tools will not be sharpened regularly, bowl blanks may be mounted when they are unevenly balanced rather than making the effort to cut off the extra waste. Once large equipment has been installed, changes to workshop layout, or improvements to equipment, are often impractical, so you look for ways to make small modifications without removing what you have already installed.

With this in mind, I should like to take you on a quick tour of my own workshop and describe some of the additions and modifications I made after I realized I should have installed things differently (see Fig 1.1). My tools include not just the mainstream kit – spindle and bowl gouges, scrapers etc – but some of the more unusual ones as well.

The lathe is probably the best place to start. I have two lathes for general turning, a short-bed lathe for bowl turning, and a long-bed lathe for spindle work. These are positioned centrally in the main working area, back-to-back. They are supplemented with a large home-made lathe, which I only use for extra-heavy work.

Often the dimensional capacity of a lathe far outstretches the stability of the machine and its fixings. You probably already have your lathe mounted on a heavy bench or a stand bolted to a suitably thick concrete floor, but its stability can be improved further still. By attaching one end of a length of steel box section to the back of the lathe, at an angle of 45°, and fixing the other end to the floor, you will increase the effective size of the base of the lathe (see Fig 1.2). The box section can be easily obtained from most local welding and fabricating engineers.

Depending on how tall you are, you may need to increase the height of the lathe if you have a machine with an integral pedestal. If the lathe is likely to need repositioning at a later date, a platform can be made out of heavy steel 'I' beams. However, once you have decided on a permanent position, a base cast in concrete will provide even more stability (see Fig 1.2).

Tool storage

Having the lathes back-to-back means I can store the equipment I use most often, such as chucks and drivers, in the area between them. My central storage area consists of two carousels mounted in a couple of flat bearings (see Fig 1.3). The top shelf, containing the chucks, has ⅝in (16mm) dowels fixed vertically to prevent the chucks falling off when the shelf is rotated. It is important that any storage facility is positioned so that you do not have to reach across the lathe, when it is switched on, to access it.

Fig 1.2 *A length of steel box section fixed between the back of the lathe and the floor increases the effective size of the lathe base, and thus increases the lathe's stability. Note the use of a separate, foot-operated stop switch which I have fitted on all my lathes.*

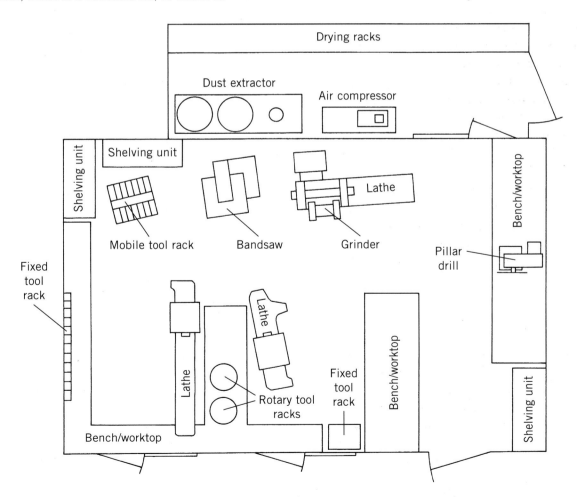

Fig 1.1 *Workshop layout. Make sure you leave enough room around the lathes to stand when using the longer tools for turning hollow vessels or deep bowls. The window between the workshop and dust extractor shelter allows the warm air extracted to be circulated back into the workshop.*

Fig 1.3 *A rotary shelf makes a useful storage area when space is at a premium.*

Fig 1.4 *A mobile tool rack is a valuable asset.*

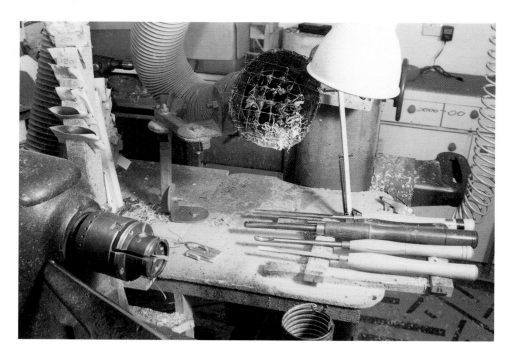

Fig 1.5 *A movable arm enables the extractor hood to be sited in any position. Below the hood is an extendible tool rack which has a series of 'V' grooves to prevent the tools rolling around. When not in use, this can simply be slid out of the way. Notice the sanding rack above the lathe for keeping abrasives in order.*

Fig 1.6 *Colour coding handles can help enormously if the fronts of tools are hidden.*

Having more than one machine means that I need turning tools in more than one place. To overcome this I have a tool rack on casters containing the chisels and gouges I use most often (see Fig 1.4). I made it from a wheeled chair that I obtained from a second-hand office furniture store. The tools I use least often, or only for spindle work, I house in a wall-mounted rack directly behind the lathe. When you are using the tools they need to be close at hand, either on a rack directly beside the lathe (see Fig 1.5), or on a shelf underneath the bed (see Fig 1.6).

With all the shelving around my workshop (cupboards would have been better) cleaning up can be difficult if shavings are allowed to fly everywhere. Therefore, rough turning large quantities of timber, I keep the shavings under control by hanging a couple of movable blinds behind the lathe. This prevents the shavings from filling up the shelves.

Sharpening systems

After you have sorted out the lathe, you will need some way of sharpening your tools. Whether you use a dry bench grinder or a waterstone sharpening system is a matter of personal preference. If you use a dry system, be sure to keep a trough of water to hand to cool the tools in if they overheat. Whichever system you use, ensure that it is placed high enough to avoid bending down to sharpen your tools. To save space, I have the grinder fixed to the top of my heavy-duty lathe with a quick release lever (see Fig 1.7).

Fig 1.7 *A grinder should be positioned at a suitable height. This one is secured to the headstock of a large lathe with a quick release lever. This allows it to be moved to another position when the lathe is in use.*

As far as grinding jigs are concerned, I have never been in favour of them for those who intend to turn a lot. Regrinding your tools freehand will be quicker and more effective once you learn to do it correctly. However, I do appreciate that a fingernail jig can be a useful asset to begin with. Try regarding them as sharpening aids rather than 'must have' items. If you have already become accustomed to using one, begin to wean yourself off and practise sharpening without the aid of a jig. If you use the freehand method for every second tool you sharpen, you will soon get the hang of it. Sharpening freehand has many advantages, including the speed of the process. You will be able to vary the cutting action of tools by altering the angle of bevel as it goes around the tool and you will be more sensitive to what is happening at the end of the tool. By reducing the pressure you exert on the end of the tool, not only will you prevent it overheating, you will also be able to create a finer finish which will cut better and hold its edge longer.

Dust extraction

When you first began turning, you were probably quite happy just wearing a small dust mask. Unfortunately, dust masks are seldom adequate and should be upgraded to a powered respirator as soon as possible. This will provide eye, face and lung protection all in one. You should also consider obtaining suitable equipment to remove dust directly from its point of origin.

In a small workshop the most useful dust extractors are those that can be moved around on castors. A large, wall-mounted extraction fan is often suitable for smaller workshops, however, in cold weather it can make heating the workshop expensive.

For larger workshops, a permanently fixed system linked to each machine with steel piping (plastic piping should be avoided as it can generate static electricity, thus causing a risk of explosion) may be more appropriate.

If you have the space, consider siting the extractor outside the main workshop in a separate shelter. This will prevent any dust that bleeds through the filters from circulating around the workshop, and if you make a filtered vent between the two, the warm air can then be recycled in the winter months.

Once the extractor has been sited, various machines must be connected. A lathe needs to be fitted, with a hood to direct the dust into the pipe.

This will need to be moved around for maximum efficiency, and to keep it out of the direct line of shavings or the extractor bags will fill up very quickly. For this I use a self-supporting arm (see Fig 1.5). This enables me to move the hood easily to any position in an instant. A secondary hose allows me to collect dust from the other side of the lathe at the same time. This is particularly useful when power sanding.

Saws

As you begin to turn more wood, you will want to cut your own blanks: while ready-prepared blanks are convenient, they are costly. A bandsaw should be next on your shopping list. Choose a saw with the largest depth of cut you can afford, and check that it has the power and stability to match its dimensional capacity. You may decide that because you only turn bowls up to 3in (76mm) deep, a bandsaw with a cutting depth

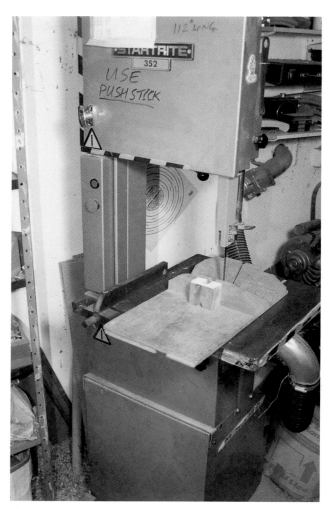

Fig 1.8 *Having a bandsaw is a huge advantage – the larger the better. Note the use of the V block for cutting round-section timber.*

Fig 1.9 *If you are going to handle larger sections of timber you need to be able to cut it. An electric chainsaw is best for workshop use.*

of 4in (102mm) will suffice. However, remember that when you begin to convert your own timber, you may find that you are offered chain-sawn blocks in 6in (152mm) thick sections.

With large bandsaws a dust collection point is normally included, but for most models this will have to be fitted. I welded a length of 3in (76mm) tube to a flat plate and screwed it underneath the saw table near the lower blade guides. The extraction pipe simply pushes onto it.

As soon as you get your bandsaw, make up a large V block. This is needed to support round-section timber and stop it rolling into the blade (see Fig 1.8).

As you begin to take on more timber, you will find that planks need first to be reduced in size in order to make them manageable. For this rough sizing I use a chainsaw (see Fig 1.9). Away from the workshop I use a petrol-driven saw, but in the workshop I use electric chainsaws. This is not just because of the danger of exhaust fumes in a confined area. A petrol-driven engine is not designed to be started and then stopped shortly after, which is what tends to happen around

the workshop. Also, an electric chainsaw is much lighter and more manageable for small work, and the noise level is lower.

If you are going to use a chainsaw, it is essential that you obtain the necessary training (see Useful Addresses, page 207) and *always* wear suitable protective clothing – hard hat with ear defenders, rip stop trousers and steel-capped boots – even for occasional use. Of course, if you are only cutting small planks, then an alternative is to use a large circular saw or one of the alligator style saws.

With the number of power tools used in a workshop, trailing cables can be a problem. If you install extra sockets on the ceiling above the benches, you will find that much of the cable is kept clear of the work area. The addition of a circuit breaker should also be considered.

Holding equipment

The most basic of equipment must be the two- and four-prong drive centres used with either a dead centre or a revolving (live) centre (see Fig 1.10).

Fig 1.10 *Different drive centres. Clockwise from front: parallel shank drive for mounting in chuck jaws; BCWA four-prong light-pull and mini drive; standard four- and two-prong drives; large, home-made two-prong drive with dovetail mounting; Robert Sorby multi-head revolving centre with wooden plugs fitted. A wooden sleeve can also be fitted over a standard centre, but the heavy duty revolving centre is necessary for larger work.*

Fig 1.11 *From back left: three-jaw chucks with home-made dovetailed jaws; BCWA 2½in (64mm) multi jaws and 1¼in (32mm) pin jaws fitted on Axminster four-jaw chucks; chuck keys, long reach, standard and extra short; 1½in (38mm) mini jaws; square-socket self-tapping screws with driver, for use with 2¾, 3½, and 4½in (70mm, 89mm and 114mm) faceplates.*

Moving on from these, faceplates are available in a variety of sizes, although nowadays I only use faceplates for larger work and tall, hollow vessels. If you use faceplates a lot, then a powered screwdriver used with square-socketed, self-tapping screws will be of great benefit.

Over the years there have been various types of collet chucks available to woodturners, providing a cost-effective way of holding the work. However, as most of these need two levers to tighten the chuck onto the work, and there is a lack of movement in the jaws, they are better suited to the occasional user. For the more serious woodturner a self-centring four-jaw chuck is the best option. I can use the Axminster

four-jaw chuck, with its wide range of accessories available from various manufacturers, for almost everything (see Fig 1.11).

Tools

By now, no doubt, you will have put together a basic collection of tools; bowl and spindle gouges, parting tools, skew chisels etc. To begin with, many wood-turners feel that if a tool is a certain shape when they buy it, then that is probably the best shape for that tool – but the best shape at the end of a particular tool is a matter of individual preference. This is unlikely to be anything like the shape of the original tool, especially with spindle gouges (see Fig 1.12), so

Fig 1.12 *Differently shaped ⅜in (10mm) spindle gouges. From left: side and top profiles as supplied by the manufacturer; side and top profiles after regrinding to suit my needs for general use.*

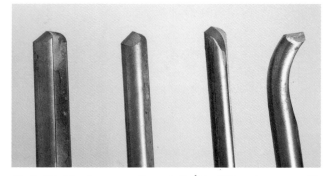

Fig 1.13 *Bowl gouges. From left: ½in (13mm) gouge with short 25° bevel; ⅜in (10mm) gouge with long, 45° bevel; ⅜in (10mm) gouge with extended side bevel; and ⅜in (10mm) angled bowl gouge.*

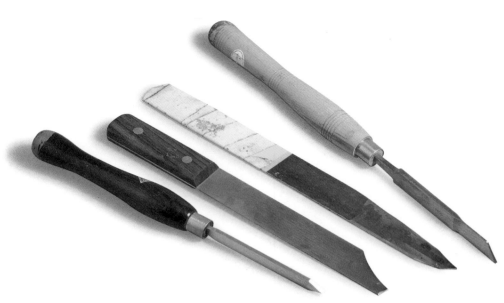

Fig 1.14 *From left: I use the standard ⅛in (3mm) parting tool for turning steps and shoulders; the ¹⁄₁₆in (1.5mm) wide Melvyn Firmager parting tool or a home-made parting tool (made from a power hacksaw blade) when wood removal needs to be kept to a minimum; and a ³⁄₃₂in (2mm) BCWA fluted parting tool to leave a good finish.*

experiment for a while, and try different shapes to see how they perform in different situations.

I keep two sets of bowl gouges in the three main sizes, ¼in (6mm), ⅜in (10mm) and ½in (13mm), with each set ground differently. One is ground with a short bevel for roughing out, or working a long way over the tool rest. I also use the short bevel when turning hard exotic woods, as a long bevel would soon lose its sharp edge if used for this purpose. The other set is ground with a longer, 45° bevel. These I use only for finishing cuts (see Fig 1.13).

I also have other bowl gouges, ground with extended side bevels, which I use when I am working in restricted areas or for taking larger cuts. Gouges with a side bevel can also be used for some of the work in hollow vessels. If I am finishing inside the

bottom of a deep bowl, I use an angled bowl gouge. If a standard gouge is used, the side of the bowl could restrict its access and prevent the bevel from rubbing. This would reduce your control over the tool and result in a poor finish.

My collection of parting tools is probably larger than most. In addition to the standard ⅛in (3mm) parting tool, I keep various other tools for different applications. I rarely use the standard ⅛in (3mm) tool for parting. Instead I keep it for such things as turning parallel steps and shoulders. For most parting cuts I need a good finish on the work with a minimum waste of wood, so I use a thin, fluted parting tool. For making small boxes or working on other items where access is restricted, I use a narrow tool, ¹⁄₁₆in (1.5mm) wide (see Fig 1.14).

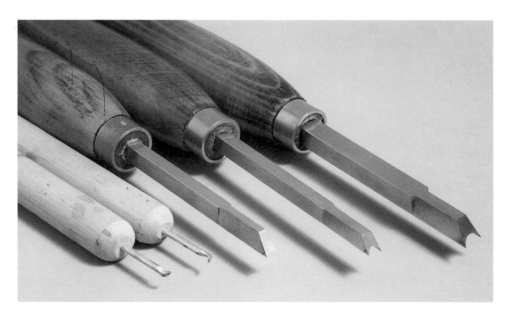

Fig 1.15 *From left: home-made ring tools (made from masonry nails); BCWA fluted bead forming tools.*

Many woodturners favour a skew chisel for turning beads. When I started out I could never get on with the skew, so I made some bead forming tools instead. While I am now happy to use a skew chisel I still prefer to use a forming tool to cut a bead as I find it much quicker (see Fig 1.15).

Hollow turning is an area that many turners are still wary of – something I intend to put right in this book. A whole number of strange looking tools have been developed over the years, many of which I have borrowed and tried. But at the end of the day I still prefer to hollow out a vessel with the simple, angled tools based on the early cranked designs made popular by David Ellsworth.

For most rough hollowing, a straight tool is all that is needed; even a modified bowl gouge will do. It is only for undercutting and finishing cuts that angled tools are necessary (see Fig 1.16).

Finishing materials

When I travel around the country demonstrating and exhibiting my work I am constantly asked how I obtain such a fine finish. The quick and honest answer is preparation. Fine sanding followed by a good polish applied to a clean surface. A lot of good work is let down because the surface has not been cleaned thoroughly before the finish is applied. While some of the dust can be removed with a tack cloth, there is no substitute for compressed air when it comes to cleaning. This is especially true when working on coarse-grained woods. If you are only an occasional turner you do not have to rush out and buy a compressor. Compressed air is available cheaply in canisters, either as a pressurized air duster from office and computer equipment suppliers, or as an air brush propellant from art or hobby stores.

The type of finish is a matter of personal taste. Some prefer an oiled finish, while others, including myself, prefer a sanding sealer and wax finish. As long as the surface has been well prepared you are halfway there. Coarse woods can be sprayed with a mist of water to raise the grain, then given a further sanding. Any areas of bark in the surface will need to be scrubbed clean using a small wire brush.

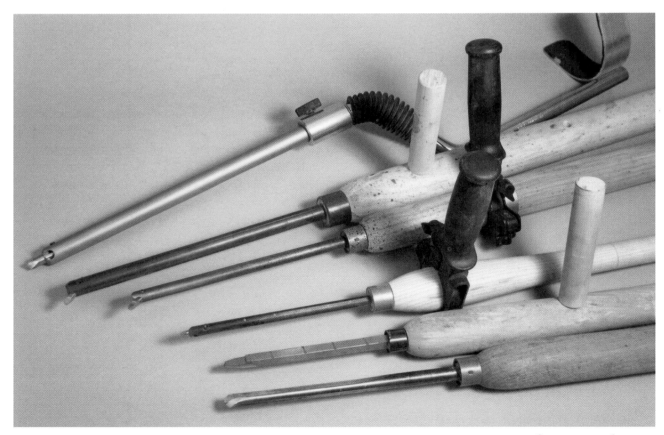

Fig 1.16 *Hollow turning tools. From front: bowl gouge with long side bevel; rough hollowing Mole; ³⁄₈in (10mm), ¹⁄₂in (13mm) and ⁵⁄₈in (16mm) twin-position, angled hollowing tools; ³⁄₄in (19mm) twin-position hollowing tool in arm brace. Note the power drill grips used as top handles.*

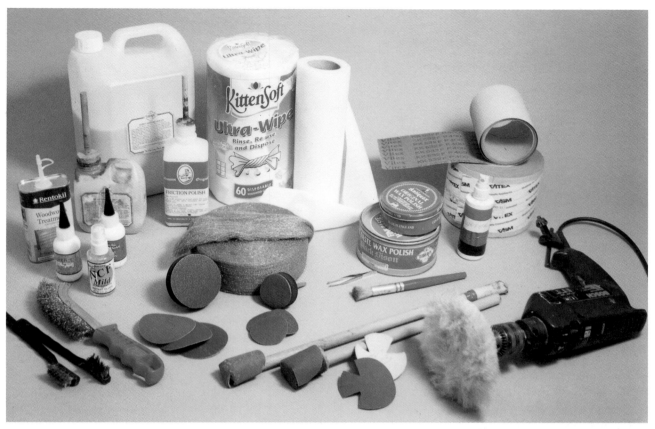

Fig 1.17 *My finishing kit includes: 'Hot Stuff' (cyanoacrylate glue), used to stabilize soft areas in the wood; woodworm fluid (just in case); power sanding discs and home-made sanding sticks; various waxes, sanding sealers and friction polishes (the brushes are kept in the bottles with wooden corks for stoppers, so you never need to wash them out); lamb's wool bonnet for rapid polishing; and water spray to raise the grain before final sanding.*

Sanding need not be laborious, as a whole host of power sanding attachments are available. If the inside of a bowl or vessel is difficult to reach safely, a sanding stick can be made. Take a length of dowel, glue a piece of foam to one end and cover this with a strip of sticky-backed velcro. Velcro sanding discs can then be cut to shape and attached to this (see Fig 1.17). A good quality, flexible abrasive is important. Choose a variety that does not cause excessive heat build-up. This is particularly important when sanding end grain. If you tear the abrasive from a roll, make sure you have some way of identifying its grit size when it is stored away (see Fig 1.5).

After the applied finish is dry, the surface must be cut back. For most large items I start with 0000 grade wire wool and finish with 1200 grit silicon carbide paper. For small items or bowls with a bark edge, on which wire wool could become caught up, I use only the paper. I apply wax with wire wool. Using too much pressure when polishing is a common mistake. If too much force is used the wax will be flattened off. This leaves a dull finish and may also cause the wax to build up on the polishing cloth where it will quickly harden, and in this state will cause scratching on the surface of the work. On large areas this scratched effect can be reduced by using a rotary lamb's wool bonnet for buffing (see Fig 1.17). If a high sheen is required, the wax should be buffed with a minimum of pressure.

The type of cloth used for buffing is also important. A soft cotton cloth will give a good shine but could easily become caught in the work. A soft paper cloth is better: if it catches it will simply tear away instead of wrapping around the work. Any cloths used for applying oiled finishes should be disposed of or kept in an airtight container. If left in the open they are liable to spontaneous combustion. Wire wool should also be stored carefully. It should be kept away from grinders and shavings: sparks from a grinder could set it on fire, and if it becomes contaminated with shavings it must be discarded or it will scratch the surface of your work.

2 obtaining and working WITH TIMBER

A STUDY OF DIFFERENT TIMBER SPECIES would require a whole book on its own. However, as this book covers rather more examples than most, I have included an index of those mentioned in order to help you find them quickly. (See Index of Timbers, page 209.)

When working with exotic woods, and with some European woods, you must be careful to control your exposure to the dust. Many species can cause allergic reactions. Symptoms include nose, eye and skin irritation, and sometimes more severe complaints such as respiratory problems. All of these can be avoided if

1 Sonokeling
2 Masur birch
3 Claro walnut
4 Cedar
5 Madrona burr
6 Amazon rosewood
7 Spalted beech burr
8 Hairy oak
9 York gum burr
10 Palm tree
11 Gutta percha
12 Spalted box
13 Zebrano
14 Papua New Guinean ebony
15 Kingwood
16 Pink ivory burr
17 She oak
18 Gimlet burr
19 African ebony
20 Santos rosewood
21 Cocobolo
22 Australian tiger myrtle
23 Osage orange
24 Thuya burr
25 Bocote (Mexican rosewood)
26 Manzanita burr
27 Pink gidgee
28 Oregon tiger myrtle
29 Amboyna burr
30 Rio (Brazilian) rosewood
31 Tulipwood
32 Rippled musk
33 Snakewood
34 Eucalyptus burr

Fig 2.1 *Colour variations in different timber species.*

Fig 2.2 *The variation in colour between heartwood and sapwood can be very decorative when used for natural-edged work, as this trio of laburnum bowls illustrates. Retaining the bark on the centre bowl makes the contrast even more striking.*

good dust extraction is provided and a suitable mask, or a powered, air-fed respirator is worn.

Colour

There are so many different species of timber, variations in colour are vast, ranging from pure white timbers such as holly to the blackness of ebony, and from the soft yellow of pequia through to the dark red of padauk (see Fig 2.1). Most woodturners will only ever encounter a few of the many thousands of species available. I have experienced around 150 different woods, some exotic, others indigenous.

Some woods are quite bland in colour. Many European woods, such as sycamore and even oak, can look comparatively plain so I usually reserve them for larger designs that show off the figure better. Some of the more exotic timbers, on the other hand, are very striking, with a variation of figure that can be clearly seen even in small items (see Fig 2.1).

Woods that have contrasting colours between heartwood and sapwood can be used to dramatic effect. They can make very attractive natural-edged bowls as the line of colour change follows the profile of the rim. This characteristic is found in many exotic woods and in a few European timbers, including laburnum, yew and sometimes elm (see Fig 2.2).

I am often asked if I have a favourite wood. I guess, if I am honest, I have several. All have different properties and some are more suited to certain designs than others. If I was forced to use only one species, I

Fig 2.3 *If iron is present in yew wood, such as this piece of wire shown by the arrows, the surrounding timber will turn purple. Quite a contrast to the original golden colour of the piece on the left, which was cut from the same log.*

Fig 2.4 *Yew can be one of the most varied woods, often displaying a whole range of colours and patterns within one small area, as this natural-edged bowl cut from the crotch illustrates.*

would probably choose yew. There can be such diversity of colour and figure within a single yew tree, and I know of no other species that can boast such wonders. Sometimes you will be fortunate enough to find a piece with iron inside. This reacts with the tannin in the tree to turn it purple (see Figs 2.3 and 2.4). As well as its appearance, I am also fascinated by the mystery associated with the yew including folklore through the ages, magic and rituals that are now nearly forgotten, even healing powers, both spiritual and scientific – drugs used to treat cancer have been made from the yew.

Figure

You will often hear people say 'what an attractive grain', when what they are referring to is 'figure'.

Fig 2.5 *Prepared blanks of maple illustrating ripple (left) and quilted figure (right).*

Fig 2.6 *The rare quilted pattern on this large olive ash platter can only be described as stunning.*

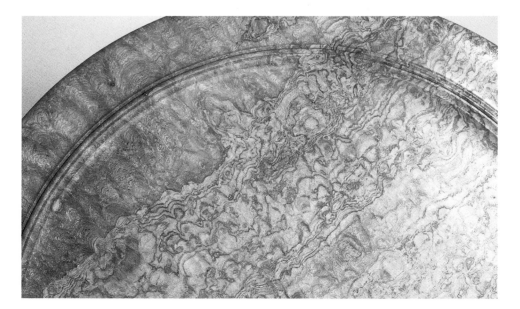

Fig 2.7 *A fine example of a rippled pattern.*

Grain refers to the structure of the wood, the longitudinal arrangement of the fibres within the tree, while *figure* refers to the surface effect, the pattern on the face of the wood when it is cut. Changes in grain structure can have an effect on figure; rippled figure and quilted figure are caused by wavy grain (see Figs 2.5, 2.6, 2.7 and 2.21j). Flame or crotch figure (sometimes referred to as feather) is caused by the grain dividing, which occurs where the tree branches into two (see Fig 2.8). When woodturners refer to highly figured timber, it is normally burr wood that comes to mind. This is another effect caused by a change in the grain; burr wood occurs where there is a concentration of dormant buds, or knots, which often show as wart-like growths on the outside of the tree (see Figs 2.21d and 2.25).

Some figure is determined by the way the wood is cut, the most common methods being plain sawing and quarter sawing. Plain sawing is essential for rippled and quilted woods in order to capture the figure at its best. Quarter sawing is preferred when working timbers with strong medullary rays, such as plane (referred to as lacewood when quarter sawn) and oak, as the boards will then have a series of silvery streaks (the pattern of the medullary rays) running across the grain.

If a bowl is turned from a quarter sawn board the grain will run in parallel lines across its surface. In some woods this can be attractive, though woods with very bold stripes are sometimes better suited to plain sawn boards as the stripes may conflict heavily with the form of the work (see Fig 2.21e). If a shallow bowl is turned from a plain sawn board with the top of the bowl towards the outside of the tree, the figure will show as a series of graceful elliptical rings. If the bowl is positioned the other way within the board a different effect is achieved. Try it.

Fig 2.8 *An example of flame figure.*

15

Other more unusual effects can be achieved by using growths from pollarded trees. Pollarding is the regular pruning of a tree's main branches to a height of about 6–8ft (2m). Historically, trees were pollarded to provide small, harvestable branches out of the way of grazing animals; today pollarding is practised more for aesthetic purposes. Pollards give a figure similar to burrs but the knots are fewer and larger, with many areas of bark and dead wood (see Figs 2.9 and 2.10).

The roots of a tree will produce a wild, unpredictable figure, but obtaining them is often difficult. Trees that have been blown down, or removed as part of a building development, are the best source as in these cases the whole tree is often uprooted. Walnut and yew roots are particularly useful, displaying a wide range of different colours. The ball of the root contains areas of twisted, swirling grain interlocked with bark pockets. Mineral deposits in the soil will often stain the wood producing wonderful effects. Some species will even produce a burr within the root making them even more desirable (see Figs 2.11 and 2.12).

Spalting

The term 'spalted' is applied to timber that has been attacked by fungal growth. The black lines are a result of two different fungi meeting and reacting in the wood, rather like erecting a fence to protect their own area and keep it from being invaded. Spalting is most likely to occur when timber is lying in warm, damp conditions such as those found on a forest floor. Beech, maple, ash, birch and sycamore are some of the more commonly affected species. Always wear a respirator when working unseasoned spalted woods, as the fungal spores remain active until the timber has dried out. Some fungal spores are a health hazard and can cause respiratory problems if inhaled.

If you are fortunate enough to come across a tree with naturally-occuring fungal growth, then treasure the find, as naturally spalted timber is always best. On occasion I create my own spalted wood (see Fig 2.13). Once the wood has been cut into blanks, I soak them overnight in a large water butt, adding a quantity of liquid plant feed. The next day I wrap the blanks in clingfilm (plastic wrap) so that the moisture is retained until they are ready to use. If a blank is rough

Fig 2.9 *Pollards, like this sycamore, offer something a little different. With care and patience some wonderful ragged designs can be created. However, the large amounts of bark and dead wood they contain make them rather fragile to work.*

Fig 2.10 *These vessels, in sycamore, illustrate the unusual effects that can be created from pollards.*

Fig 2.11 *If a challenge is required, try cutting into the root of a tree. Inside this Australian mallee root, is a whole range of colour and twisted grain.*

Fig 2.12 *This Australian mallee root is quite hard, but with sharp tools results are possible.*

Fig 2.13 *These beech blocks were all cut from the same part of the tree and wrapped in clingfilm for six months. The two square blocks were first soaked in a mix of liquid plant food, the large disc was soaked in plain water and the small disc was wrapped without soaking (its moisture content at the time was 24%).*

Fig 2.14 *The spalting on this partially burred beech was created after the blank was rough turned.*

Fig 2.15 *(Close-up of Fig 2.14.) While the spalting is not very deep, it has produced a very even effect.*

turned before being soaked and wrapped, the effect can be quite different. In this case, the black zone lines will often follow the contours of the design (see Figs 2.14 and 2.15). In addition, as the spalting does not have as great a depth of wood to penetrate, results can be achieved much quicker.

As soon as the wood is sufficiently spalted, remove the wrapping and dry the work. Once it has dried to below about 20% moisture content, the fungus will no longer be active and the wood will be safe to work. If the wood is left damp for too long, the spalting will advance and the fibres will become too soft to work.

Obtaining timber

When first starting out, most woodturners are able to satisfy their timber demands quite easily by purchasing ready-prepared supplies from their local stockist. However, once the woodturning bug bites hard you begin to use more and more timber. You find the local dealer does not carry the range of timber you require or is simply too expensive for larger quantities, so you have to look further afield to satisfy your requirements.

While you are unlikely to obtain large quantities of free timber, you should certainly be able to make sizeable savings on merchant prices. Where you look will depend on what your requirements are. Small blocks of timbers such as ash, oak and maple are usually readily available from shop fitters and local joinery firms. They will be using large quantities and often have to cut short lengths, which are of no use to them, from the ends of their planks.

You may require small ornamental trees such as lilac or sumach. Try placing an advertisement where gardeners are likely to read it, for example, in the parish news, in garden centres or in local shops. If you want laburnum, place an advert with local playgroups and nurseries. Parts of laburnum are extremely toxic and most parents will be happy to have the trees removed when their children begin to walk.

For burrs, cankered woods and other odd lumps, tree surgeons are the best source. As well as felling whole trees they will often be asked to remove growths and single branches. Generally of no interest to the saw mills, these smaller pieces are ideal for woodturners. I once sent a mailshot to local tree surgeons listing the different species and types of figure I was interested in. As a result of this, I am still contacted on a regular basis with offers of different woods and unusual lumps.

Tree surgeons will often have to fell trees in back gardens where access to machinery is restricted. If they are unable to remove the butt whole they have to cut it into small, manageable blocks. Such butts are often cut into rings for firewood, but if you are willing to pay, most tree surgeons will happily cut them into useful slabs instead.

Planning consent is often required if mature trees need to be removed for a building development, so keep an eye on local planning applications for any trees that are being felled. Developers normally just want to get the tree out of the way so that they can begin work. Another useful place to look is *Woodlots*. This bi-monthly magazine, published by the Forestry Commission, carries information on a wide range of timber for sale in both large and small quantities (see Useful Addresses, page 207).

You may feel that a whole butt is too much, and once you build up a few contacts you'll soon find that you're offered more than enough timber for your needs. If you are a member of a local woodturning group (see Useful Addresses, page 207) why not divide the timber, and the costs, amongst you.

Felling

Once you have located your tree you may have to fell it or have it felled. First, you must check whether or not a felling licence (available from the Forestry Authority) is required or if the tree is subject to any restrictions such as a Tree Preservation Order (TPO) or Site of Special Scientific Interest (SSSI). For most smaller trees, and for those in gardens, a felling licence isn't normally necessary, but it's always wise to check with local authorities first as regulations do have a habit of changing. When felling larger trees, always call in the professionals (see Fig 2.16). If you are going to use a chainsaw to fell the tree yourself, make sure you have the correct safety equipment and attend a course detailing its safe use (see Useful Addresses, page 207). If not, get someone else to do it.

Smaller trees can be cut down with an axe or bowsaw but the method remains much the same. Look for any lean or heavy branches on one side of the tree to determine the direction of fall, then clear all

Fig 2.16 *Professional help is required for felling larger trees. The large branches must be removed before the tree is felled. If they are left, the tree may break its back when it lands, wasting much of the valuable timber.*

Fig 2.17 *You must identify an escape route and clear it of any obstruction before you begin felling. The hinge at the end of the felling cut helps the tree fall in the right direction.*

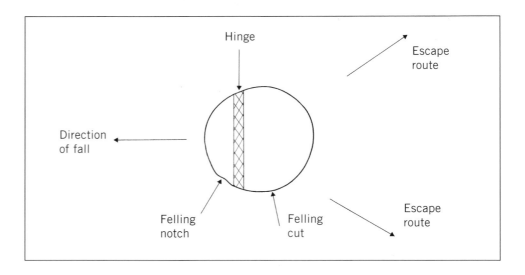

obstacles from around the tree and establish an escape route. This should be on the side opposite the direction of fall, at about 45°, in case the butt of the tree jumps back when falling (see Fig 2.17).

Using your axe or bowsaw, cut a *felling notch* in the side on which the tree is to fall. This notch should be a wedge-shaped section cut to a depth of about one-quarter of the tree's diameter (see Fig 2.18). The *felling cut* should be made horizontally, opposite the notch, and about 2in (51mm) higher (see Fig 2.19). Continue cutting until the tree begins to fall or until a hinge of about one-tenth of the tree's diameter is left between the felling cut and the notch (see Fig 2.17). If you reach this point, stop and drive wedges into the cut to tip the tree over: if you continue to cut

through the hinge you will not be able to control the direction of fall.

Rough conversion

After you have felled the tree you need to cut it into manageable pieces. For large trees it is best to have the tree cut into planks by a sawmill (see Fig 2.20). The exceptions to this are heavily burred trunks and butts that are of an uneven shape. If you are able to use a chainsaw safely, or know someone who can, such trees are best cut selectively to get the best out of the figured areas. It will help if you have a basic understanding of what can be produced by cutting different parts of the tree in different ways. Figure 2.21 illustrates some of the different effects possible.

Fig 2.18 *The felling notch is cut in the side on which the tree is to fall.*

If haulage is a problem, the wood will need to be converted into chain sawn blocks on site. Ideally these should be kept as long as possible to allow for some end checking (cracking across end grain) of the timber. Alternatively, if the wood is coarse and straight grained, oak and ash being good examples, cut it into short lengths slightly longer than the diameter of the tree. These can then be split in two with wedges driven into the edge of the block and, if necessary, split again into quarters. Small flitches are easier to manage and are useful for different bowls and vessels (see Fig 2.22). The flitches should be placed in sacks to prevent the ends from cracking or the whole blank will be lost due to its short length.

The branch wood should not be discarded. If it is large enough it can be used for small bowls and spindle work, although with any branch wood there will be more stresses in the fibres than in the butt. Because branches grow at an angle from the trunk, the fibres in the upper side of the limb are in a state of tension, while those in the lower side are in a state of compression. These forces lead to the development of *reaction wood*. In the northern hemisphere this is formed in the upper side of the limb in hardwoods and the lower side in softwoods. The reverse is true for trees in the southern hemisphere. Reaction wood can be difficult to work with: items made from it will often move unevenly as they dry, which must be allowed for, and it is sometimes difficult to obtain a smooth finish. Many pieces are left with a woolly appearance which requires further attention.

Fig 2.19 *The felling cut is made opposite and slightly higher than the notch.*

Fig 2.20 *Most sawmills will be happy to plank whole butts to suit your requirements.*

Fig 2.21a *Laburnum. Diameter: 5in (127mm). By using the crotch of the tree, a feathered effect is produced.*

Fig 2.21b *Acacia. Diameter: 5¾in (146mm). Positioning the burr at the base of the bowl gives the illusion of a separate pedestal.*

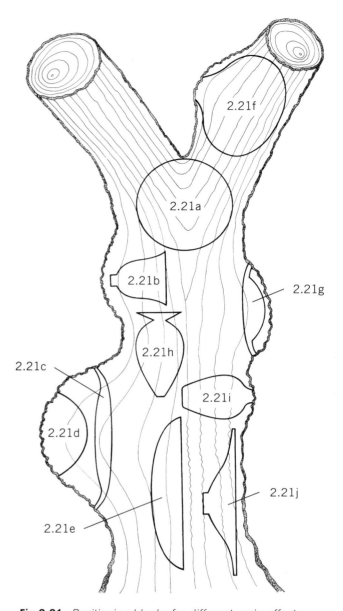

Fig 2.21 *Positioning blanks for different grain effects.*

Fig 2.21c *Eucalyptus burr. Diameter: 28in (711mm). By taking a flat slice right through a large protrusion, a full burr figure is possible.*

Fig 2.21d *Elm burr. Diameter: 7½in (190mm). This is the most common positioning of bowls using burr. The base of the bowl will display the face figure, while the edges will show the figure as long streaks reaching towards the rim.*

Fig 2.21e *Zebrano. Diameter: 11in (279mm). A bowl from a quarter sawn board will give a striped effect. This position is most suited to timbers with strong medullary rays. Beware when using boldly striped woods, as the pattern can sometimes conflict heavily with the rounded form of the bowl.*

Fig 2.21f *Hairy oak. Diameter: 5½in (140mm). The use of the whole section of branch in this hollow vessel allows the contrast of sapwood and heartwood to be exploited. The medullary rays are clearly visible, radiating out from the centre pith.*

Fig 2.21g (top view) *Yellow box burr. Diameter: 13in (330mm). Positioning the bowl across an oval burr gives a combination of burred heartwood and less pronounced sapwood is achieved.*

Fig 2.21g (side view) *Placing the base of the bowl towards the outside of the tree, the rim can be turned back on itself to give the effect of water overflowing.*

Fig 2.21h *Ash burr. Diameter: 5in (127mm). If a vase is turned parallel to the axis of the tree (along the end grain), the growth rings will follow the form of the work when viewed from one side. This often accentuates the profile of the design. Viewed from the other side, the grain will remain vertical and evenly spaced, giving the vase a thinner, taller appearance.*

Fig 2.21i *Cherry burr. Diameter: 5¼in (133mm). When a vessel is placed on its side within the tree (along the cross grain), the growth rings form gentle, wave patterns around the diameter and can be used to suggest movement. The horizontal lines will make a piece appear shorter and fatter, and this must be taken into account when turning the profile.*

Fig 2.21j *Rippled eucalyptus. Diameter: 8in (203mm). If the grain is rippled or quilted, the best effect will be achieved turning a shallow bowl from a plain sawn board. If a rippled log is quarter sawn, the figure will be severely reduced.*

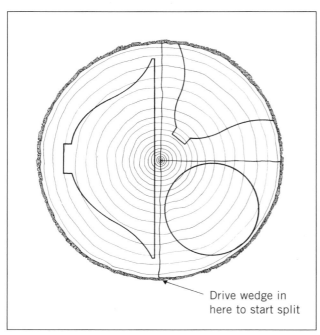

Drive wedge in
here to start split

Fig 2.22 *Short sections of log can be split into rough blocks with wedges if a chainsaw is not available.*

Final preparation

Once converted to planks, or rough blocks, the butt must then be further reduced. With boards or large chainsawn slabs, this task is relatively straightforward. First cut a thin slice off the end to help identify the position of any cracks in the wood. Study the surface and look for any bark pockets, any holes and any areas of particular interest, and decide how these should be used or avoided. Outline the position of the blanks on the blocks in coloured chalk. I often try a number of variations, using a different colour outline each time, until I am satisfied that I am getting the best out of the wood (see Fig 2.23). The next thing to decide is

where to cut first to ensure that you don't have to cut through one blank to remove another. Again, I mark these lines out in a different colour.

With the plank reduced to manageable pieces, I cut out the blanks using a bandsaw (see Fig 2.24). When cutting wood on the bandsaw never use excessive force: if you have to push hard on the wood, it is time to change the blade. Be sure to keep your hands and fingers out of the line of the blade at all times – even when your hands are several inches away. Imagine that every piece of wood you cut has an invisible crack starting just in front of the blade and running out to the edge of the wood. One day you will find such a piece. When a blade meets such a crack, the wood will break away and you will suddenly jerk forward, but having been forewarned, you will be clear of the blade.

Fig 2.24 *For creating your own blanks, the bandsaw is invaluable.*

Fig 2.23 *After studying both sides of the board, I mark on the position of the blanks in chalk. The white lines indicate the position of the first cuts, the yellow lines highlight bark inclusion or cracks in the wood.*

Fig 2.25 *Position the blanks to extract the best quality pieces, not the highest quantity, and take care to ensure that the rim of the work will look roughly balanced when it is finished.*

Burrs and bark edges

A slightly different approach is needed for preparing bark-edged blanks. Assuming you have a large section of timber to work with, study the log carefully and see where the best areas of figure will be. Look also at the high and low points along the surface. If you wish to make a natural-edged bowl, consider how the blank could be most effectively positioned in order to capture the best figure and at the same time create a balanced edge to the work (see Fig 2.25). If the natural edge is not positioned evenly to the rim of the bowl, the end result is that one side of the rim will be lower than the other, creating a slanting effect. Once you have marked the position of the bowl, cut this section from the log. If possible, try to make the cut at 90° to the face of the blank.

Once the blank has been removed, it can be further reduced using the bandsaw. The first step is to provide a flat base that is parallel to what will be the top of the work. If a flat base is not created then the blank may not have any support under the point of cut. An unsupported cut will cause the work to tip into the blade with disastrous consequences.

With the bandsaw switched off, line the work up so that the two opposite sides of the blank are parallel to the blade, then cut the base so that it is flat and parallel to the rim (see Fig 2.26). Once the base flat is created, the corners of the blank can be sawn off. A rough circle is good enough as the lathe will soon bring the blank into balance.

If you are using a ready-cut blank from your timber merchant then most of this will have been done for you. The drawback with using pre-cut natural-edged blanks is that not only are they often cut with a

slanting top edge, they may well have been cut from the log without full consideration given to the position of the blank in relation to the best figure available. After all, the timber merchant needs to get the largest number of blanks from a log in the shortest possible time to make his money. If you cut blanks yourself you can, and should, aim for a lesser number of better-figured blanks.

Seasoning and storage

Once you have collected your timber, be it boards or logs, it must be stored correctly to allow it to season. If the timber is in boards then it should be put into stick (stacked flat with spacers between the boards at

Fig 2.26 *With the bandsaw switched off, line the blank up so that the two opposite sides of what will be the rim are parallel to the blade before sawing the base flat.*

18in (457mm) intervals) until you are ready to use it, preferably out of the sun and under cover. The exception to this is sycamore which should be stood upright (end reared); if not, the wood will dry with black blotches in it. While the timber should be kept out of the wind, some airflow is necessary to help prevent the growth of mildew. The ends of the timber should be painted with either a liquid wax or a 50% solution of PVA glue and water to prevent the ends checking (cracking).

To speed up the seasoning process, I rough turn most of my work and then put it under cover to finish drying naturally. I have never liked working with kiln-dried timber as it is very dusty and lifeless. If the work is particularly wet, I seal the end grain with a PVA solution and keep it in a cardboard box or a sack for the first six to eight weeks. This slows down the drying process and prevents the piece from cracking, especially with burr woods. The box must be opened regularly to allow a change of air and prevent mildew. After this, I remove the work from the box and leave it on a drying rack in a covered shelter for a few more months. Finally, I bring the blank into the workshop and keep it up high, in the warm air, until fully dry.

When work is rough turned and allowed to dry afterwards, it must be left oversize to allow for shrinkage and movement in the wood. The amount of movement will vary depending on the size of the work and where the wood was cut from the tree (see Fig 2.27). The most-stable blanks are those cut from a quarter sawn board, or a square section cut equally about the centre line. Blanks cut from a plain sawn board or a square-section cut in the quadrant of the tree will move quite considerably.

As you gain experience you will know when work is dry, but to begin with you will need to check. The most reliable method for this is to use a moisture meter to measure the exact percentage of sap left in the wood. Alternatively, weigh the part-turned work periodically and record its weight each time. When the weight is stable the work is as dry as it is going to get within its current environment, although not necessarily fully seasoned. Wood can only be as dry as its surroundings.

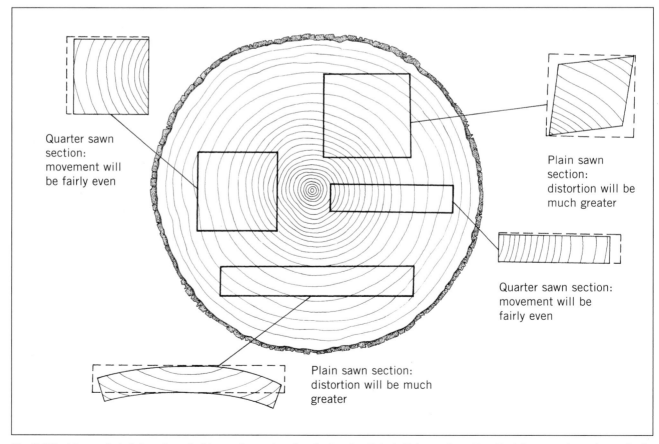

Quarter sawn section: movement will be fairly even

Plain sawn section: distortion will be much greater

Quarter sawn section: movement will be fairly even

Plain sawn section: distortion will be much greater

Fig 2.27 *All wood shrinks when it dries out causing the timber to distort. It is worth noting that for round-section spindle work the shrinkage will produce almost exactly the same oval effect regardless of where the blank is cut from.*

PART TWO

Lidded Pots and Boxes

in preparation

Take the trouble to look through museum collections and you will see a whole range of turned lidded containers from the past. With lidded finial pots, even the overall effect has remained much the same for a very long time; a central container adorned with an intricately turned stem or pedestal. The main difference in more contemporary designs is that the function of the piece often takes second place to its aesthetic appeal.

It is clear when you look deeper into the designs around today that their origins go way back. Some are influenced by early wassail bowls, others by past designs of chesspieces. Ceremonial chalices also share similar properties. Whatever is your influence, you are bound to enjoy the exploration of different shapes. Woodturners past and present have been drawn to the complexity of these designs, and with every turner who has ever approached the subject, another variation is born. Once you have grasped the basic techniques involved there will be no limit to the variations you create. But to give you some ideas to start, a number of examples are shown in the first Gallery (see page 77).

Design

The designs of the pots and boxes you work on will be influenced by a number of factors. The first must be your level of skill, as this will determine how challenging the project should be. By changing a few elements of the design, you can tailor the projects to your own level of proficiency. If you are a relative beginner, you may wish to increase the stem thickness

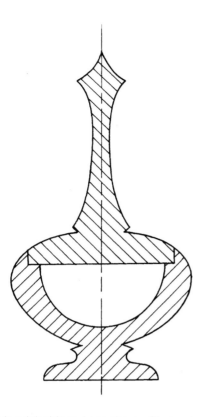

Fig 3.1 *It is advisable to keep the profile as simple as possible until you gain a little more confidence.*

addition, if the box is completely free from any bead details or other surface decoration, the relationship between the base and the lid will be more important.

The intended use of a pot and, if you sell your work, your customers, may also have an effect on the design. If the finished piece is to be functional, or is to be sold at craft shows, it is better to have a more stable design. A thicker stem will be more robust, and a stout foot, with the bowl of the pot positioned close to the base, will help keep a pot from being knocked over. However, if you wish the pot to be purely decorative, or are going to sell your work through galleries, a finer design is possible (see Fig 3.2).

Boxes, while still decorative, are inherently more functional as they have a wider base in relation to their height, and are thus far more stable.

The fit of the lid must also be considered. If a pot is to be functional, the lid should be easily removable with one hand while a closer, sliding fit would better suit a more decorative box. However, a lid should never be tight or any slight movement in the timber will cause it to jam.

of a pot to as much as ½in (13mm) in diameter, and maybe shorten its length slightly. Details on finials should also be kept simple, and pedestal feet could be shorter and thicker to begin with. You could even increase the thickness in the bowl until you gain a little more experience (see Fig 3.1).

With lidded pots the position of the bowl relative to the overall height of the pot will affect not only the stability of the pot, but also how the eye views it. If the bowl is turned at the end of a long stem with a very small finial on the lid, it may appear unstable, whereas if the bowl is too far down, or has no pedestal at all, it can appear dumpy and lifeless.

Boxes are considerably more substantial and stronger than lidded pots and, as they have no slender stems to break off during turning, it may be argued that they are more suitable for beginners. A box may have elaborate detail around the joint and decorative lines on the lid, or could be as simple as a flat-topped cylinder with no detail at all. However, it is worth noting that while the more complicated profiles of finial pots will partially disguise any errors in proportions, the simpler designs of boxes will merely emphasize any errors in the flow of the lines. In

Fig 3.2 *Amazon rosewood pot. Height: 4½in (114mm). If the pot is to be purely decorative, a more delicate design is possible.*

Timber

Assuming you wish to create a pot with a reasonably fine stem, a close-grained hardwood is preferable. Beech, hornbeam, laburnum and most of the straight-grained exotic timbers are particularly suitable, but avoid woods with interlocking or woolly fibres. Some timbers, such as olive, may have a hidden wavy grain structure which will cause them to snap when turned to a small diameter, though their use will provide a greater challenge should you require it.

For flatter, domed boxes there is a much wider selection of timbers from which to choose. Their stoutness means that coarser woods such as oak and elm, and with care even the palm woods, can be used (see Fig 3.3). Generally, boxes are turned with the grain running along the axis of the work, as are the taller pots. This provides greater stability in the fit of the box, as there is less movement of wood across the end grain than across the side grain. However, with care, a box can be made with the grain set across the work as for bowl turning. If you are following the projects in this book, this just means that you will be working in the opposite direction on some of the cuts.

Setting the grain across the box can be particularly useful for timbers with heavy medullary rays, such as oak and plane (lacewood), or those with a radiating figure, as in masur birch and snakewood. The only drawback is that the timber must be allowed to stabilize for a longer period. If this is not done the lid and base may bow.

Fig 3.3 *Coconut palm. Diameter: 3in (76mm). By keeping the design simple it is possible, with care, to use one of the more fibrous woods as with this box.*

Practice

In the following few chapters I'd like to share with you some of my interpretations of finial pots and boxes, although I'm sure many will have been made at some stage before.

There are a number of techniques common to all the designs. I have listed these below and suggest you spend a little time studying and practising them before starting on the projects.

Select a fairly low speed while practising – mistakes always cause more damage at higher speeds. Practising now will allow you to concentrate on the individual projects without being distracted by the supplementary, but equally important information.

Woodturning should be enjoyed, so there is little point in rushing into a project that is too difficult. This will only cause frustration and dent your confidence. Just work at your own pace. Your level of enjoyment will increase as you learn. As you progress and feel more confident, you will soon find yourself creating designs with more finely turned stems and crisper, more delicate details.

As you become more adventurous, you will want to create new shapes. Use scrap wood from the firewood pile and turn the intended profiles into the surface. This will allow you to see how the finished pot will look and avoid spending time turning a completed pot only to find you don't like it, although it could be argued that such experimentation is a good opportunity to practise tool technique.

Mounting the blank

Look for any markings in the figure before deciding on the best orientation for the pot or box (see Fig 3.4). When mounting between centres, I prefer to use a revolving, hollow ring centre made by Robert Sorby tools (see Fig 3.5) rather than a conventional 60° centre, as there is no centre point to damage the fibres of the wood. Alternatively, if you are using a standard centre, glue a scrap of wood to what will be the top end (see Fig 3.4). When making domed boxes you will need to glue a scrap of wood to both ends to prevent the centres damaging the work. If this is not done, not only will the centre leave an indent in the wood, the fibres in front of it will be crushed (see Fig 3.6). This often results in the need to turn away as much as ¼in (6mm) of damaged wood – an expensive mistake when using some of the exotic timbers.

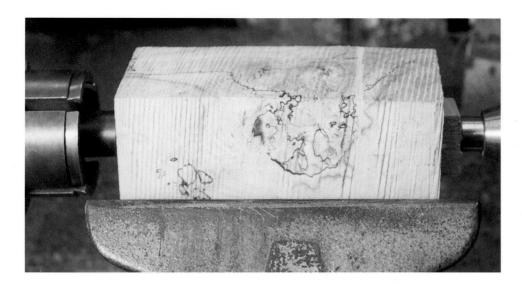

Fig 3.4 *Look for any markings in the figure to decide where to place the top of your piece. Glue a scrap of wood to this end to prevent the fibres of the blank from being crushed by the centre.*

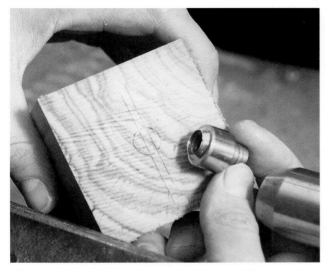

Fig 3.5 *By using a hollow-cone centre, the fibres at the middle of the blank remain undamaged.*

Fig 3.6 *This square pot was supported with a conventional 60° centre, and the damage caused to the end is clearly visible.*

Seasoning

Most air-dried native timbers and part-seasoned exotic timbers still have a moisture content upwards of 14%. To overcome this, pots and boxes need to be part-turned and set aside to finish seasoning. This is just a matter of keeping them in a dry environment until their moisture content is down to around 10%. For most native timbers this will normally take a few months, but for very dense timbers, such as lignum vitae or snakewood, it can take anything up to two years. Even dry wood needs some time to stabilize. If this is not allowed, the natural stresses in the timber, which are released once the wood is cut, may cause the work to move slightly, which will have an effect on the fit of the lid.

The time required for seasoning can be frustrating, especially when you are eager to get on and finish your pots and boxes, but if you ignore this advice on rough turning and seasoning, it will be at your peril. To avoid future frustrations, when you rough out the blank between centres, ready for holding in the chuck jaws, rough out some extra blanks at the same time. You can put these aside to dry while you are working through the other projects.

Rough hollowing the bowl

As this process is common to all end-grain pots and boxes, I suggest that you take a little time to practise the method on some scrap wood before starting on any of the projects.

First a hole must be drilled to the required depth. Using a spindle gouge, turn a slight hollow in the centre of the work to allow the gouge to be entered safely. Set the tool rest so that the tip of the gouge is cutting on the centre line. With the flute uppermost, push the gouge slowly into the work until the correct depth is achieved. You will need to withdraw the tool periodically to clear out shavings that build up.

My preferred method of hollowing end-grain pots is to use the back hollowing technique, using a ⅜in (10mm) spindle gouge with a 45° bevel angle. This is done by entering the gouge a short way into the hole, with the flute angled away from you at about 45° to the horizontal. The handle should also be at 45° from the face of the work and in a horizontal position (see Fig 3.7). Begin the cut by lowering the handle and

rotating the flute away from your body in a clockwise direction (see Fig 3.8). As you work around the inside, lower the handle, moving it to the left towards the headstock as you go, and continuing to rotate the flute away from your body. As you near the outer edge of the bowl, the bevel should still remain in contact with the wood. At the end of the cut you should finish up just before the 2 o'clock position. Repeat the cut until the bulk of the waste has been removed.

Hollowing the pot in this way, removing the wood from the upper right area of the pot, may take a while to become used to, but for removing waste quickly, it is by far my favourite method. It produces a true cut

Fig 3.7 *To rough hollow the pot, angle the flute of the spindle gouge away from your body at 45°. The handle should also be at an angle of 45° from the face of the work and in a horizontal position at the start of the cut.*

Fig 3.8 *As you begin the cut, lower the handle and rotate the flute further away from your body as the tool moves around the inside. You should finish up at the 2 o'clock position with the bevel still in contact with the wood.*

Fig 3.9 *The spindle gouge may be used in a scraping method to rough out the inside. Swing the handle away from your body as you bring the tip of the tool out towards the edge.*

which is always more efficient than scraping the wood, and the tool rest becomes a leverage point making the cut almost effortless. The only drawback is that you don't have quite as much control over the process as with the scraping method, which is why I use the latter for the final finishing cuts.

If, after practising on scrap wood, you find you are still having difficulty with this, you may prefer to rough out the pot using a spindle gouge and the scraping method as for the finishing cuts. To do this, hold the gouge with the tip cutting just above the centre line, and have the handle raised very slightly above a horizontal position with the flute facing you at an angle of 45°. Enter the hole and push the handle away from you as you bring the tip of the tool out towards the edge, using your fingers against the tool rest as a pivot point (see Fig 3.9). Repeat these cuts until the bulk of the waste is removed.

Cutting the recess for the lid

Once the hollow has been roughed out, the recess for fitting the lid into the base must be turned. (For boxes, the recess will be in the lid.) For this task I use a ½in (13mm) square-ended scraper, ground with a 90° form set round at an angle of 5–10° to the tool (see the detail in Fig 3.10).

Set the tool rest so that the tip of the tool is cutting slightly above the centre line. With the scraper held flat against the rest, turn the recess a mere ¹⁄₃₂in (1mm) deep at this stage (see Fig 3.11). It should be turned so that the diameter stops just

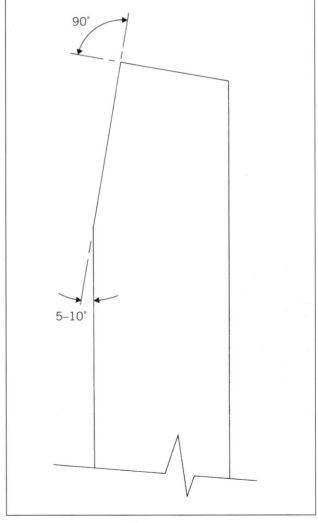

Fig 3.10 *Top view of a ½in (13mm) scraper ground with a 90° angle set at 5–10° skew.*

33

short of the small witness of a step on the face of the work (see Fig 3.12). This small witness is the edge of the shoulder on the mating part that is deliberately left attached when the two halves of a box are parted through. By keeping the depth of recess shallow at this stage, if you make a mistake and remove too much from the diameter, you will need only to turn away a very small amount in order to remove the error. If you turn the recess to the full depth in one go and make the same mistake, you will either have to scrap the pot or be left with a poor-fitting lid.

Check the fit by offering the lid (for boxes this will be the base) to the recess and then continue the cut until the lid just fits. Now turn the recess to depth, working in small stages and checking the fit regularly as you go. The diameter of the recess can be increased very slightly to produce a close but not tight-fitting lid. This allows for any slight movement caused by changes in temperature or humidity after the pot is completed.

Making a start

Now that you have a basic understanding of the groundwork, you are ready to begin turning. The projects are arranged, as much as possible, in a basic order of progression, but if you wish to start with the square pot, or the domed box, go ahead. If you do get stuck, just refer back to the previous chapters for additional information.

Throughout the book I make many references to the use of a ⅜in (10mm) spindle gouge. This size is merely my own preference; you may find it easier to use a ¼in (6mm) spindle gouge when turning some of the finer details.

Fig 3.11 *Keep the scraper flat against the rest and above centre line while cutting the recess for the lid.*

Fig 3.12 *By turning a shallow recess of only ¹⁄₃₂in (1mm) to begin, if you do cut oversize you will often be able to correct your mistake rather than scrap the pot altogether. Note the small witness of the lid that is left attached to the base.*

basic
LIDDED POT

Pau rosa. Height: 3¾in (95mm).
Diameter: 1⅞in (47mm).

IF EVER A TURNED ITEM WAS DESIGNED for holding your thoughts and wishes, the lidded pot must surely be it. In this first project I shall explain in detail my techniques for making these pots.

Preparation

To begin, prepare a blank 2in (51mm) square and about 4in (102mm) long, depending on your intended design. To turn any item in wood you need to see the finished piece in your mind so you can lay out the correct proportions in the wood. After all, if you can't see it, you can't make it. For some this is easy, for others it will come with experience. For now, I suggest you pencil the position of the main details onto the blank to act as a rough guide.

Roughing out

Mount the work between centres and rough the blank to a cylinder using a 1¼in (32mm) roughing gouge – ¾in (19mm) would suffice – with the flute angled into the cut at 45°. Once this is done, shape the basic form of the pot with the ¾in (19mm) roughing gouge (see Fig 4.1). Reduce the profile further using a ½in

Fig 4.1 *The basic form of the pot is turned using the ¾in (19mm) roughing gouge.*

Fig 4.2 *A dovetail mounting to suit your chuck is turned on the base. The drive centre held in the chuck allows the size of the dovetail to be easily judged by eye, using the diameter in the jaws for comparison.*

(13mm) spindle gouge, leaving the pedestal at least an 1in (25mm) in diameter, to support the work later. Finally, using either a ⅜in (10mm) beading and parting tool or a 15° form tool, turn a dovetail mounting on the base of the pot to suit your chuck (see Fig 4.2). If you are able to mount the drive centre directly into the jaws that will later hold the work, you'll find it easier to gauge the size of the dovetail by eye without the need for any measuring. At this stage the work needs to be put aside to finish seasoning.

Refining the shape

After the wood has seasoned, remount the work directly into the chuck jaws. While the logical step would be to start turning at the tip of the finial and work back, I prefer to start by establishing the main bowl of the pot first because everything else is positioned in relation to this.

Using a ⅜in (10mm) spindle gouge, start the cut at the fullest part of the blank. Turn away the wood in one continuous movement to produce a smooth curve towards the lid. Keep the gouge tilted over on its side, so that the cutting edge is about 10° from vertical, to produce a fine shearing cut, requiring only a minimum of sanding later (see Fig 4.3). Repeat the cut for the underside of the bowl, leaving the lower stem area as it is, to support the hollowing later.

The next step is to turn the flat shoulder or tennon of the lid, using the tip of a conventional parting tool (see Fig 4.4). Leave a small shoulder at

Fig 4.3 *A fine, shearing cut is produced with the side of the gouge, leaving a clean cut surface.*

Fig 4.4 *The flat shoulder of the lid is turned using the tip of a parting tool. Care must be taken to ensure that this is parallel.*

Fig 4.5 *A ³⁄₃₂in (2mm) fluted parting tool is used to mark the position of the base of the lid, leaving a small witness from the shoulder attached to the base of the pot.*

the top of the bowl around ¹⁄₃₂in (1mm) deep. If this is not done, the rim of the bowl will end up with a sharp corner when it is hollowed out. At this stage the width of the flat should be in excess of ¼in (6mm). Take care to ensure that this is turned parallel or it will affect the fit of the lid.

Before turning in the detail of the finial, use a ³⁄₃₂in (2mm) fluted parting tool to mark the position of the base of the lid, cutting to a depth of ⅜in (10mm) (see Fig 4.5). Leave a small witness from the shoulder of the lid attached to the base of the pot. This will act as a guide later, when you turn the recess for the lid. If you are using a parting tool made from an old power hacksaw blade with the teeth removed, or any other parallel-bladed tool, remember to open up the cut slightly: the tool will bind in the cut if this is not done.

Now, roughly shape the upper face of the lid leaving the shoulder about ³⁄₁₆in (5mm) wide.

Detailing the lid and finial

After turning away the scrap wood that was used to protect the end, the next step is to turn in the fine spindle for the top of the finial. Using the spindle gouge, remove some of the waste wood from the stem to give a diameter of around ⁵⁄₁₆in (8mm). Face off the end of the tip at 45°. This will prevent the fibres breaking away when you turn the tip to a fine point. Keeping the gouge on its side, gently turn away the wood from the top of the finial to give a slight taper (see Fig 4.6). Fine cuts are necessary to ensure that you don't snap the wood.

Leaving a small flat, ⅛in (3mm) wide, for the bead detail, rough turn some of the waste from the lower end of the stem. To turn in the bead there are a number of different methods. My preferred method, wherever possible, is to use the end of a fluted parting tool (see Fig 4.7) or a fluted bead forming tool (see Fig 1.15, page 9). Alternatively, you can roll the bead with the point of a skew chisel. For fine work such as this, you could even use the side corner of a conventional parting tool in the same way you would use a skew chisel. With the bead detail turned, lightly chamfer the corners either side, using the long point of a ½in (13mm) skew chisel (see Fig 4.8).

Now turn the lower end of the stem to size with the spindle gouge. Starting just below the bead, turn the top end to produce a tight curve leading down

Fig 4.6 *Keeping the gouge on its side, gently turn away the wood from the top of the finial to give a slight taper.*

towards the stem diameter. Continue the cut for a length of about ½in (13mm) and repeat until you reach the finished size. Next, turn away the lower end of the stem, blending it in so that the diameter tapers out slightly towards the bottom end (see Fig 4.9). At the base of the stem, between the stem and the rough face of the lid, you should leave a step ¹⁄₁₆in (1.5mm) wide and with a diameter of ½in (13mm).

Using the spindle gouge, take a light cut across the face of the lid to give a gentle curve that harmonizes with the curve on the bowl of the pot. By keeping the gouge right over on its side a fine shearing cut is possible (see Fig 4.10). Don't present the tip of the tool straight into the wood or you risk tearing the fibres of the end grain.

Create a small 'V' in the step using the long point of the skew chisel to cut each side, and blend it into the face of the lid (see Fig 4.11). Alternatively, if the use of a skew chisel sends a shiver up your spine, these small 'V' cuts can also be made using the tip of a ¼in (6mm) spindle gouge with a long bevel angle (see Fig 10.10, page 102).

Sanding and finishing the lid and finial

Now, gently sand the lid, being careful not to soften the crisp details of the work. Sanding down to 400 grit is normally sufficient, unless you are turning one of the dense, exotic woods. It may then be necessary to go down as far as 800 grit or fine lines will be visible on the finished piece. If you use cloth-backed

Fig 4.7 *The small bead is turned using the end of the fluted parting tool.*

Fig 4.8 *The long point of a ½in (13mm) skew chisel is used to lightly chamfer the corners of the bead.*

Fig 4.9 *The spindle gouge is used to turn away the stem so that the diameter tapers out towards the bottom end.*

Fig 4.10 *By keeping the gouge right over on its side, a fine shearing cut is possible, even on end grain. Note the finish left behind the gouge.*

Fig 4.11 *A small 'V' is created in the step using the skew chisel.*

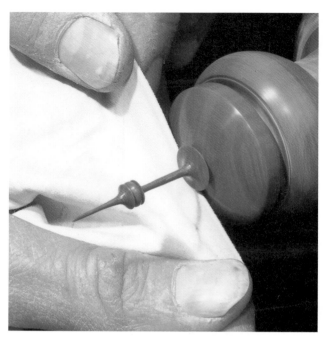

Fig 4.12 *Polish the fine detail gently with the edge of a folded cloth.*

abrasives, make sure there are no loose threads: they could wrap around the work and snap the stem. When sanding end grain you will often find that the fibres of the wood become slightly raised when it is polished. This can be avoided if the surface is lightly moistened, after sanding to 320 grit, using a fine spray of water from a small, pump action container (see Fig 1.17, page 11). This will raise the fibres which will then be cut off during the final sanding.

With the lathe stationary, apply a coat of sanding sealer or friction polish with a brush and remove any surplus with a soft paper cloth. Use this cloth to lightly friction dry the surface.

After cutting back the surface, apply a soft wax paste. If you are using wire wool, stop the lathe while applying the wax to the finial or it will wrap around the stem. With the wax applied, bring the lid to a low shine with a soft cloth. By keeping the cloth folded and pulled tight, you can use the edge to get into the fine grooves along the work (see Fig 4.12).

Finally, cut off the lid using your thinnest parting tool. Mine is made from a $\frac{1}{16}$in (1.5mm) wide, toothless, power hacksaw blade, with masking tape over the end for the handle (see Fig 1.14, page 9). Fortunately, similar tools are now available commercially (see Useful Addresses, page 207).

Because you made the positioning cut for the lid with the $\frac{3}{32}$in (2mm) parting tool, you will now have enough clearance to use the $\frac{1}{16}$in (1.5mm) blade to part off the lid at a slight angle. This will produce a small hollow in the underside of the lid and remove some of the excess weight.

As your cut nears the centre of the work, gently support the lid with your hand to prevent it flying across the workshop (see Fig 4.13).

If you are still gaining experience, stop the lathe when the cut nears the centre and use a fine hacksaw blade to cut through the remainder. Put the lid aside, ready for finishing later.

Fig 4.13 *Support the lid by hand as the parting cut nears the centre of the work.*

Fig 4.14 *For maximum efficiency, rough out the bowl with the ³⁄₈in (10mm) spindle gouge, using the back hollowing technique.*

Hollowing the base

Rough hollow the bowl of the pot with a spindle gouge (see Fig 4.14), using the back hollowing technique described in Chapter 3 (see Figs 3.7–3.9, pages 32 and 33). Once the bowl has been rough hollowed, cut the recess for the lid using a ¹⁄₂in (13mm) square-ended scraper (see Fig 4.15). Turn the recess to size in stages until the fit gives a smooth flow between the base and lid of the pot, as described in Chapter 3 (see Figs 3.11 and 3.12, page 34). The recess should not be too tight or any slight movement

in the wood after the pot has been finished will cause the lid to jam. Now remove the remaining wood from inside the pot, using the spindle gouge in a scraping method. Hold the gouge with the flute facing you at 45°. Pick up the cut in the base of the bowl and push the handle away from your body as you bring the tip of the tool out towards the edge. Ideally, the bowl of the pot should be turned to an even thickness of around ³⁄₁₆in (5mm), leaving the lid recess about ¹⁄₈in (3mm) wide. If necessary, the inside surface of the pot can now be refined further by shear scraping, using a

Fig 4.15 *The recess for the lid must be turned gradually to ensure that it is not cut oversize.*

Fig 4.16 *A ¹⁄₂in (13mm) round-nosed scraper can be used to shear scrape the inside of the bowl to refine the surface finish.*

¹⁄₂in (13mm) round-nosed scraper. Shear scraping involves using the scraper with the blade twisted to one side so that the cutting edge is slightly over on its side to give a finer cut. The tool rest should be set so that the tip of the tool is cutting slightly above the centre line in a trailing motion (with the handle higher than the cutting tip). Start the cut at the centre of the bowl, with the top of the blade inclined anticlockwise by about 10°. As you swing the handle out to the right, rotate the tool further to the left to an angle of about 45°, bringing the tip of the tool around the inside and out to the edge as you go (see Fig 4.16). Cutting by this method leaves a very smooth surface requiring only a minimum of sanding.

Rough turning the pedestal

Using a spindle gouge, rough the upper area of the pedestal down to ¹⁄₂in (13mm) in diameter. Keeping the gouge on its side, as described on page 36, blend in the underside of the bowl to meet the top of the pedestal. Rough turn a little more from the foot, to around ⁵⁄₁₆in (8mm) in diameter, before incising a small 'V' at the underside of the bowl (see Fig 4.17).

Sanding and polishing the bowl

Before proceeding any further, I advise you to sand and polish the bowl of the pot. If you leave this until you have finished turning the stem, it may not be strong enough to resist the drag from the abrasive,

Fig 4.17 *After the pedestal has been rough turned, a small 'V' is incised in the underside of the bowl with the skew chisel.*

which may cause the stem of the pedestal to snap. When sanding the inside of the bowl, tear off just a small piece of abrasive, ½in (13mm) wide, and fold it in half lengthways. This will make it easier to gain access to the tight corners inside (see Fig 4.18).

Refining the pedestal

After sanding and polishing the bowl, mark the position of the base of the foot using the ³⁄₃₂in (2mm) fluted parting tool, leaving a central diameter of about ¾in (19mm). This base should be turned as close to the chuck jaws as you feel comfortable with, which

will depend on your level of experience. With this done, the base diameter can then be turned to size with the spindle gouge.

Finish the stem of the pedestal using either the ³⁄₈in (10mm) or ¼in (6mm) spindle gouge. Working in stages from both ends of the stem, turn away the wood until you reach the required diameter. This base stem should be left slightly thicker than the stem of the lid, both to give a balanced appearance and to provide the strength necessary to support the finished piece (see Fig 4.19). When finished, the stem should have a tight curve at both ends. If the lower stem is very

Fig 4.18 *When sanding the inside of the bowl, tear off just a small piece of abrasive and fold it in half. Supporting one hand with the other will give you greater control.*

Fig 4.19 *The stem of the base is left slightly thicker than that of the lid to give a balanced look to the finished piece.*

Fig 4.20 *Turn away the foot to within ¹⁄₁₆in (1.5mm) of the base to produce a sweeping concave surface.*

Fig 4.21 *This tiny shoulder in the rim around the base will give your work more interest.*

Fig 4.22 *When parting off the base, use the fluted parting tool. This will leave a clean surface requiring only a minimum of sanding.*

thin, you may need to provide extra support as

thin, you may need to provide extra support as described in Chapter 5 (see Fig 5.11, page 52).

Depending on how long you have made the pedestal, you may find that access to this area is restricted and extreme care must be taken. You need to be aware not just of the position of your fingers, but also where the wings of the spindle gouge are in relation to the concave ends of the stem. If the upper cutting edge touches the side of the stem, a dig-in is likely, and with a fine pot such as this, the stem will probably snap.

You should now be left with an area for the foot about ½in (13mm) wide. Keeping the gouge on its side, turn away the base of the foot to within ¹⁄₁₆in (1.5mm) of the parting cut made earlier (see Fig 4.20). Work first in a concave curve, then blend the foot into a convex surface where it meets the base of the stem. Using the skew chisel, turn a small 'V' between the stem and the foot of the pot. Next, make a tiny step in the rim around the base of the foot, using the corner of a conventional ⅛in (3mm) parting tool (see Fig 4.21).

Sanding and polishing the pedestal

Finally, sand and polish the pedestal, being careful not to damage the crisp edges you have turned. When parting off the base, you must support the work with one hand as the cut nears the centre (see Fig 4.22). The small pip left in the centre can then be removed

with a small carving gouge. After parting off, sand the undersides of the base and lid, using a sanding disc held in the chuck jaws (see Fig 4.23). A light application of sealer and wax polish on the undersides, and the pot is complete.

Fig 4.24 *Finished project in Pau rosa.*

Fig 4.23 *The undersides of the base and lid are sanded using power sanding discs.*

Next steps

Once you have created this basic pot, there are many extra finishing touches you can add as you become more confident. For example, the underside of the lid and base can be reverse-turned as described in Chapter 19 (see page 196). Finials can be made more elaborate, and pedestals made taller. Captive rings can be added as described in Chapter 5 (see page 53). The possibilities are endless. Just work at your own pace and set your own targets as you go.

5 square-edged LIDDED POT

Tulipwood. Height: 5¼in (133mm).
Width of flange: 3in (76mm).

AT FIRST GLANCE, MUCH OF THIS square-edged pot may seem very similar to the basic pot in Chapter 4. They each have a stemmed pedestal, a finial at the top, and a lid that is recessed into the base, so you could be forgiven if you assume that the turning methods are the same. However, having a square rather than a circular flange around the bowl, which is also set higher up the stem than on the pot described in Chapter 4, changes not only the appearance, but also some of the ways in which the pot is made. A square lip will restrict your access to the finial when turning and, as the surface of the square flange is turned before the lid is parted off, the finial prevents the tool rest sitting close to the area being worked.

As mentioned in Chapter 3, the pots can be as intricate or as simple as you wish, to suit your own abilities. For this project I would advise you to err very much on the side of simplicity until you gain experience. A flange width of at least ¼in (6mm) around the square edge, and very basic decoration upon a stem of ½in (13mm) or more is not unreasonable for your early attempts.

Preparation

Start with a blank about 6in (152mm) long and from 2½in–3in (64–76mm) square. Within reason, the design can be made from any size blank, but if you work with anything less than 2in (51mm) square, the pot loses some of its visual impact as the square lines around the top will be less significant.

I would like to stress that with any square-cornered project rotating at speed there is always the danger of injuring yourself. If you are in any doubt as to your ability to tackle this project, I suggest you come back to it once you have progressed a little. A good introduction to working irregular edges is to practise on a few simple, shallow, natural-edged bowls, or begin by choosing an octagonal shaped box as described in Chapter 7 (see Fig 7.1, page 62).

Roughing out

Find the exact centres of the work prior to mounting in the lathe, as any errors will result in the square edge of the pot being lopsided. My preferred method is to use a marking gauge and run it along all four edges. This will leave a small box in the middle, from which the centre can be easily found. Alternatively, you could mark across the diagonals.

Mark a line defining where you want the join between the lid and the base of the pot and then, with the blank secured between centres, rough turn the profile. Take care if you are using a standard ¾in (19mm) roughing gouge as you may splinter the edges of the wood, which would ruin the edges of the square

Fig 5.1 *After roughing out the profile, use the ³⁄₈in (10mm) beading and parting tool to turn the shoulder of the lid. Note the use of the hollow-cone centre to prevent damage to the end of the work.*

later on. Alternatively, you could use a ½in (13mm) spindle gouge to rough out the form around the area of the square edge.

Start by turning away some of the lid area to remove a 45° section of wood, working close, but not right up to the line in case the wood splinters. Keeping to the left of the line by about ½in (13mm), rough out the base and stem of the pot, turning down to around 1½in (38mm) in diameter – any thinner and you will not have the rigidity to support the pot for hollowing later. Don't forget to leave enough at the base to create the dovetailed fixing.

Reduce the profile further using a ½in (13mm) spindle gouge to remove some of the excess waste from the top of the lid and the underside of the bowl.

Turn a dovetail mounting at the base of the pot and rough out the shoulder for the lid with a ³⁄₈in (10mm) beading and parting tool (see Fig 5.1). Put the pot aside to finish seasoning and stabilize.

Refining the shape

After the wood has stabilized, remount the work in the chuck jaws. With the tool rest positioned across the top of the pot at about 30° to the lid of the pot, true up the top face of the square flange. In an ideal world you would start the cut at the centre of the work and draw the cut out to the edge, working with the grain. However, as access is restricted by the lid, which is still attached, I suggest that you work from the outside inwards, cutting against the grain.

Taking only fine cuts so as not to splinter the wood at the edges of the square, turn a slightly concave surface using the tip of a ³⁄₈in (10mm)

spindle gouge (see Fig 5.2). This will give a gentle curve on the square edge when the pot is finished. You will be working very close to the spinning corners at this stage, so take extreme care as to the whereabouts of your fingers.

If you have not had much experience of working with square flanges, I strongly suggest that you practise some of the cuts first. Whenever you need to

Fig 5.2 *A slightly concave surface is turned in the square edge, taking only fine cuts so as not to splinter the edges.*

Fig 5.3 *The spindle gouge is used to turn the parallel shoulder for the lid, taking care not to let the lower wing of the tool catch the surface of the square face.*

reduce square stock to a cylinder, use the waste to practise and turn a series of shoulders all the way along its length. If you do this a few times you will gain valuable experience.

Once the top face of the square has been formed, turn a parallel shoulder that will become the fitting for the lid (see Fig 5.3). The diameter of this shoulder should be at least $\frac{5}{16}$in (8mm) inside the square edge (no more than $2\frac{3}{8}$in (60mm) in diameter when using 3in (76mm) square stock). This will allow sufficient wood in the base of the pot to recess the lid into later.

You will need the $\frac{3}{8}$in (10mm) spindle gouge to turn in the shoulder as it needs to continue until it is within $\frac{1}{32}$in (1mm) of the top face of the base. The concave surface around the square would make it more difficult to use the parting tool, as for the basic pot in Chapter 4.

As the cut nears the square face, angle the gouge over so that just the tip is cutting. If you don't do this, the lower wing of the tool could catch against the square edge. Take care to ensure that your fingers do not venture too close to spinning corners. If you are worried that you will catch the tool, use an angled scraper or a 15° dovetail form tool, such as a hollowing 'Mole', to cut the shoulder (see Fig 10.4, page 100). With this you will be able to reach into the corner with less risk of catching the edge.

At this stage the shoulder should be at least $\frac{5}{16}$in (8mm) proud of the top corners of the square. Mark on the position of the underside of the lid, using the $\frac{3}{32}$in (2mm) fluted parting tool. To do this, slowly bring the side of the parting tool close to, but not touching, the top corners of the base, and cut into the shoulder to a depth of about $\frac{5}{8}$in (16mm) to mark the

Fig 5.4 *The $\frac{3}{32}$in (2mm) fluted parting tool is used to mark the position of the lid before the details are turned in.*

position of the lid (see Fig 5.4). Because the pot has square corners, I suggest that to begin with you leave a gap of at least ⅛in (3mm) between the parting cut and the square edges. Avoid using a parting tool with a cutting tip higher than the centre of the tool, as there is a high risk of it twisting into the wood and shattering the corners of the pot.

Turning the lid details

Turn the face of the lid using the spindle gouge on its side to cut the wood in a shearing action. Turn a slightly curved surface leading out towards the finial. Continue the cuts until you are left with a parallel shoulder between the parting cut and the face of the lid approximately ³⁄₁₆in (5mm) wide.

Now it's time to start adding detail to the pot and to cut the lid finial. Staying with the spindle gouge, turn the finial down to about ⁵⁄₁₆in (8mm) in diameter, then gently turn the top end of the finial down to a fine stem for a distance of ½in (13mm). Form a small bead using a BCWA, ⁵⁄₁₆in (8mm) fluted beading tool (see Useful Addresses, page 207). Start the cut at the top of the bead then, as the tool enters the wood, gradually bring the handle up, lowering the cutting edge to form the bead (see Fig 5.5). If you wish to form a smaller bead, reduce the width by moving the handle in an arc from left to right as the bead nears completion. If you are the sort who enjoys an adrenaline rush, you can always use the skew chisel and roll the bead, but beware of the square edges.

Fig 5.5 *A fluted beading tool is used to form the bead that will decorate the finial.*

Fig 5.6 *Extreme care must be taken as your fingers will be working close to the sharp, spinning corners.*

Finally, blend the face of the lid into the edge of the bead so that you create a concave surface between the two. Be very aware of the position of your left hand at this stage as you will be working very close to the square edge (see Fig 5.6). Access to this area is severely restricted so you may prefer to use a narrow, round-ended scraper as described in Chapter 18 (see Fig 18.1, page 177).

Sanding and polishing the lid

Sand and polish the lid, being careful not to allow any build-up of heat on the surface while you are sanding the end grain, as this will cause heat shakes to appear on the surface of the work. Part off the lid and put aside for finishing later.

Hollowing the bowl

You should now be left with a small step protruding from the base for about $3/16$in (5mm), depending on how deeply concave you turned the square edge. Position the tool rest square across the top of the bowl and turn away the step, using the spindle gouge, to leave a small witness about $1/32$in (1mm) proud of the surface. This will be used later as a guide for fitting the lid.

Rough hollow the bowl of the pot as described in Chapter 3 (see Figs 3.7–3.9) until you are about $1/4$in (6mm) from the small witness of the step left earlier. You may prefer to use the scraping method to hollow out the middle until you gain experience of back

hollowing, as your left hand will otherwise be perilously close to the spinning corners.

The next step is to cut the recess for the lid with a $1/2$in (13mm) square scraper as described in Chapter 3 (see Figs 3.11 and 3.12). This should be turned until the face of the lid is flush with the top of the bowl. Any mismatch and the finished piece will lose some of its appeal (see Fig 5.7). If you plan to reverse-turn the underside of the lid later, remember to leave the lid slightly proud of the surface to allow for this.

Once the fit of the lid is correct you can finish the inside of the bowl. To remove the bulk of the remaining wood, use a $3/8$in (10mm) spindle gouge in a scraping action until the width of the lid recess is about $1/8$in (3mm) wide. Further refine the finish using a $1/2$in (13mm) round-nosed scraper to shear scrape the inside as described in Chapter 4 (see Fig 4.16).

Finishing the underside of the bowl

Starting at the top of the square edge, turn away the underside of the square flange, taking small cuts at a time. Try to turn this section in one continuous movement towards the stem of the pot, until you are clear of the square edge by at least $3/8$in (10mm) (see Fig 5.8). It is important to use the tip of the tool to turn the first section until you reach a true diameter, at which point the handle can be lowered and the gouge can be used on its side to produce a shearing cut. If you try to use the side of the gouge against the square edge it can easily catch and shatter the work.

Fig 5.7 *The lid recess is turned until the face of the lid is flush with the top of the bowl.*

Fig 5.8 *Fine cuts are taken with the ³⁄₈in (10mm) spindle gouge to refine the underside of the pot. A sheet of black card placed directly behind the pot helps to define its edges.*

The edges of the square flange will be unclear when the pot is spinning. To help define the edges, place a sheet of contrasting coloured card behind the pot.

Continue turning away the underside until the edge of the square is the required thickness. When the square flange is finished, rough turn away some of the wood from the stem to allow the rest of the underside to be completed. At this stage, leave the stem of the pot with a diameter of around ⁵⁄₈in (16mm) to support the top. Check the thickness in the base of the bowl with callipers periodically to make sure you have an even section all round.

Using the long point of the skew chisel, turn a small 'V' at the base of the bowl. This will give a definite end to the bowl, providing a visual separation from the stem when the pot is finished.

Sanding and polishing the bowl

Before proceeding further, sand the bowl and square of the pot. To sand the surface around the square edge, it will help if you use a good quality, flexible abrasive such as one of the cloth-backed varieties. Take care not to leave any loose threads attached as they might catch on the work. Roll a piece into a tube, hold it

Fig 5.9 *Using two hands to hold the abrasive steady will give you more control and prevent unnecessary damage to the corners.*

½in (13mm) away from the end between the thumb and forefinger of one hand, and support it with the other to provide a stable grip (see Fig 5.9). By holding it in this way and applying gentle pressure, you will be able to sand the edge without rounding over the corners. Your fingers will also be kept a safe distance from the spinning corners. If just one hand is used to hold the abrasive, or too much pressure is exerted, you can easily slip into the wood, damaging both the pot and your fingers. Stop the lathe after using each grade

Fig 5.10 *The flat edges of the square are sanded using a 2in (51mm) disc held in the chuck jaws. Take care not to round over the corners.*

of abrasive, as there may be a few scratched areas left. These can be sanded out by hand before moving on. With the face of the square finished, the flat edges can be sanded. To do this I prefer to remove the pot from the lathe and use a 2in (51mm) sanding disc held in the chuck jaws (see Fig 5.10).

Finally, polish and wax the bowl before moving on. Use a soft paper cloth for polishing: if this does catch on the corners it will simply tear the paper instead of damaging the pot or your fingers. On no account should the paper or polishing cloth be wrapped around your fingers or disaster is sure to happen. If the cloth should catch on the corner of the spinning work, you will not be able to pull your hand away. If you use wire wool to flatten the polish or apply the wax, be sure to stop the lathe first to avoid catching the corners.

Turning the pedestal

If you intend to reverse-turn the base of the pot, as described in Chapter 19 (see Figs 19.5 and 19.6, page 198), start at the base and work towards the bowl to turn the stem details. This will ensure that the stem remains strong enough to support the turning at the base until after the foot has been completed. If you are not going to reverse turn then continue as described.

As the top of the pot is fairly large in relation to the diameter of the stem, you may have to support the bowl, especially if the stem is to be fairly slender. This is done by fitting a turned wooden plug into one of the adapter ends of the hollow centre (see Fig 5.11).

Fig 5.11 *A wooden plug is fitted to the revolving centre to support the bowl while turning the stem.*

Rough turn the stem down to a diameter of around ½in (13mm) along its length, leaving enough wood to create the foot later. Using the tip of the ³⁄₈in (10mm) spindle gouge, turn the top end of the stem, starting at the left side of the 'V' cut made earlier, to produce a small, concave radius leading into the stem. Leave the diameter slightly larger than the desired finished thickness of the stem. Continue the cut for a distance of about ⅝in (16mm), leaving plenty of room to turn a small captive ring if required.

Turning a captive ring

Using a conventional ⅛in (3mm) parting tool, turn down a square shoulder to just above the stem diameter. Move the tool to the left and turn a groove to the same diameter to leave a flange on the stem about ³⁄₃₂in (2mm) wide.

Next, turn away some of the waste wood from the lower end of the stem to provide access while turning the ring. Turn a small bead on the top of the flange either by using the radius in the end of a ³⁄₃₂in (2mm) fluted parting tool, or by using a small, fluted beading tool and moving the handle from side to side to reduce the width down to the required size.

Undercut the ring on both sides, leaving just a small amount of wood attached, using two small hook tools in a scraping fashion (see Fig 5.12). My hook tools are miniature scrapers made from masonry nails. They have small left- and right-handed hooks ground on the ends (see Fig 5.13). For captive rings with a larger section, the corners of a fluted beading tool may be used to undercut the ring. After the ring is undercut, sand and polish it before separating the ring from the stem.

Using the spindle gouge, turn the upper end of the stem to the required diameter, and blend in the remaining section left from where the ring was cut. To finish, turn the lower end of the stem to blend in.

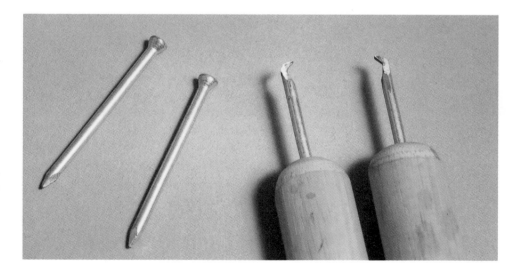

Fig 5.13 *When standard ring-forming tools are too large, miniature tools can be made from masonry nails by grinding small left- and right-hand hooks on the ends.*

Creating the foot

Turn away the waste wood, close to the jaws of the chuck, to the finished diameter of the base. Next, establish where the pot will be parted off by using the fluted parting tool to mark the base of the work. Turn in the detail of the foot before using the skew chisel to cut a small 'V' between the foot and the stem (see Fig 5.14). This should be made to look similar to the one underneath the bowl.

Fig 5.14 *Turn in the small 'V' between the foot and the stem using the long point of a skew chisel.*

Fig 5.15 *When you part off the work, the pot should be supported by the tailstock and a low speed selected.*

Final sanding and polishing

Finally, sand and polish the pedestal and stem before parting off (see Fig 5.15). Remember that wire wool should not be used on the stem while it is rotating as it is likely to wrap around and snap the work. When parting off, it is safer to select a lower speed than you have been turning at or the work could break free unexpectedly. Stop the lathe before cutting the whole way through and finish off with a fine-toothed hacksaw blade.

Sand the undersides of the base and the lid using the 2in (51mm) disc sander held in the lathe as before. Alternatively, to give a professional touch, the undersides can be reverse-turned as described in Chapter 19 (see page 196).

Fig 5.16 *The finished tulipwood pot.*

Next steps

With a little ingenuity it is possible to apply this process to other shapes, such as octagonal, hexagonal and even wavy, bark-edged pots.

6 domed BOX

Pernambuco. Height: 2¼in (57mm).
Diameter: 2⅝in (67mm).

I N THE PREVIOUS TWO CHAPTERS I dealt with fancy, intricate designs where the proportions of the base and the lid are not what the eye first recognizes. With a more formal design, you have to pay more attention to form, proportion, and the crispness of details: due to the simplicity of the shapes, these will stand out far more.

I created the pots in Chapters 4 and 5 so that their lids sat into a recess in the base of the work. For the slightly more functional design described here, the tenon is on the base and the recess in the lid. If it is made the other way around the capacity of the box will be reduced.

Roughing out

Cut a blank 2½in (64mm) long from 3in (76mm) square-section timber so that the grain runs along the axis of the work.

With the blank mounted between centres, use a ¾in (19mm) roughing gouge to reduce it to a cylinder and remove the corners at 45°. At a point approximately three-fifths up from the base of the work, turn a groove ½in (13mm) deep using a conventional ⅛in (3mm) parting tool (see Fig 6.1). Open this out to ⁵⁄₁₆in (8mm) wide, as this will later become the shoulder for fitting the two halves.

Using a ½in (13mm) spindle gouge, rough turn a slightly concave surface from a point ½in (13mm) to the right of the recess, on what will be the lid of the box. Continue the cut, leaving enough wood to create a dovetail fitting on the top of the lid to suit your chuck. For the base of the box, rough turn a convex surface. Starting about ½in (13mm)

Fig 6.1 *A ⁵⁄₁₆in (8mm) wide recess is formed three-fifths of the way up from the base of the work to a depth of ½in (13mm). Note the scrap wood block glued to the base to protect the blank from being damaged by the drive centre.*

Fig 6.2 *When cutting round-section work on the bandsaw, using a 'V' block will prevent the work rolling into the blade.*

away from the recess, turn a full radius leaving a shoulder approximately ³⁄₁₆in (5mm) wide for creating the dovetail fitting.

Staying with the spindle gouge, chamfer the edges either side of the parting cut to about ³⁄₁₆in (5mm) wide before turning the two dovetail mountings, using either the end of a conventional parting tool held over at 15° or a 15° form tool.

The two halves can now be parted through using your thinnest parting tool. Enter the tool on the right-hand side of the recess, just short of the base of the lid, so that you leave a witness of this diameter attached to the lid to act as a guide later on. Do not try to part the two halves completely. To do this you would need to open up the width of the cut to prevent the parting tool binding, and removing this unnecessary amount of wood would create a greater misalignment in the grain between the top and base of the finished box. My advice is to stop the parting cut when it reaches about ¹⁄₂in (13mm) in depth, and saw through the remaining wood.

With any round-section work, if you are using the bandsaw, be sure to use a suitable 'V' block to prevent the work rolling into the blade (see Fig 6.2). I tend not to use the bandsaw alone to separate the two halves, as there is always a small chance that the

blade could wander slightly. Again, this would cause a greater misalignment of the grain in the finished box.

Hollowing the bowl and lid

With the base of the box remounted in the chuck, position the tool rest across the face of the work. Using a ³⁄₈in (10mm) spindle gouge, rough hollow

Fig 6.3 *A ³⁄₈in (10mm) spindle gouge is used to rough hollow the box to within ¹⁄₄in (6mm) of the shoulder.*

the bowl, as described in Chapter 3 (see Figs 3.7–3.9, pages 32 and 33), to leave a thickness in the base of approximately ⅜in (10mm). Continue hollowing until you are within ¼in (6mm) of the shoulder of the lid fitting (see Fig 6.3).

Now remount the top of the box, and rough hollow the lid as you did the bowl. This should also be turned to leave about ⅜in (10mm) in the top of the lid, stopping about ¼in (6mm) short of the small step on the face of the work. This step is the tiny witness of the shoulder that was left when separating the two halves with the parting cut. Once it is roughed out, mark the two halves with a number to ensure that they are not mixed up. Set the box aside to dry and stabilize.

Refining the shape

When the box has stabilized, remount the base in the chuck. Using the spindle gouge, true up the diameter of the box, keeping the flute on its side to produce a fine shearing cut. Turn a radius from the outer diameter down towards the shoulder, leaving a step between the shoulder and the convex surface you are cutting, about ¹⁄₁₆in (1.5mm) wide and ⅛in (3mm) proud of the shoulder diameter. This step is for turning in the bead later. Now turn a gentle, convex curve towards the base of the box, stopping clear of the jaws by at least ¼in (6mm) for safety.

Form a 90° shoulder, using a conventional ⅛in (3mm) parting tool (see Fig 6.4). As for all mating parts, the shoulder should be kept as parallel as

Fig 6.4 *The shoulder is turned to about ¼in (6mm) wide with a conventional ⅛in (3mm) parting tool, making sure that the face is parallel.*

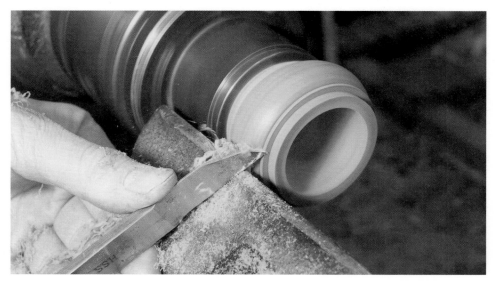

Fig 6.5 *To turn a bead smaller than the tool, move the handle from left to right to reduce the size of the bead.*

possible. With domed boxes this is particularly important as the shoulder will later be used with the lid as a friction drive when it is reverse turned.

Next, using a $^3/_{32}$in (2mm) fluted parting tool, turn a bead on the small step left earlier. This detail is an important feature of the box as it gives a strong visual break between the top and the base. As the bead is going to be smaller than the tool being used to form it, roll the top of the blade on the parting tool from left to right while moving the handle from side to side as you finish the cut – this will reduce the bead to the correct size (see Fig 6.5).

With the tool rest across the face of the work, true up the top surface of the rim before moving on to re-turn the inside of the box. Using the spindle gouge in a scraping action, as described in Chapter 3 (see Fig 3.9), lightly clean over the inside. To give a balanced feel to the box, aim for a thickness in the base of around $^1/_4$in (6mm), as the underside of the box still needs to be finished. The side should be slightly undercut to remove some of the excess weight (see Fig 6.6). The shoulder should now be about $^3/_{16}$in (5mm) thick. Refine the finish of the inside of the box by shear scraping the surface using a $^1/_2$in (13mm) round-nose scraper as described in Chapter 4 (see Fig 4.16).

At this stage, sand and polish the base of the box on the upper areas. Take care not to over-sand the

finely turned bead detail or the effect will suffer. Put the base aside, to be finished later.

Remount the lid in the jaws and, using a square-ended scraper as described in Chapter 3 (see Figs 3.11 and 3.12, page 34), turn the recess that will locate on the base of the box (see Fig 6.7). This should be turned until the base has a firm push fit; you are going

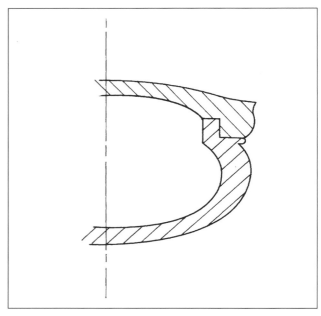

Fig 6.6 *Section showing details of the box. Note how the bowl is undercut to keep a more even wall thickness.*

Fig 6.7 *Using a square-ended scraper, turn the recess that will locate on the base of the box. This recess will also be used as a friction chuck to hold the base.*

to use this fit as a friction drive to hold the base. If anything, it is better to err slightly on the loose side. If the fit is too tight you could cause the lid to split, but if it is too loose, you can place a piece of paper cloth between the lid and base to make up the difference. Note that when turning the shallow sizing cut in the recess, the small witness on the face should not be used as a guide as it is no longer accurate. Once the recess has been formed, finish off the flat face of the lid with the spindle gouge. This will mate with the base, so it needs to run true at this stage in order to reverse turn the base later.

Reversing the base

Fit the base into the lid of the box and bring up the tailstock to lightly support the work and prevent it popping off. A flat-ended adapter in the revolving centre is preferable as it will prevent any damage to the surface of the wood. Alternatively, if you are using a 60° centre, place a small piece of scrap wood over the end to stop the centre denting the wood.

Position the tool rest across the base at about 30° and, taking light cuts, turn the dovetail fitting away. Round off the base, using the side of the gouge to produce a clean shearing cut, blending it in with the curved surface turned earlier (see Fig 6.8). Once most of the base has been turned, remove the

tailstock support to give access to the underside. When making these final finishing cuts, take care not to become over-confident or you may cause the base to slip in the lid, or even pop out of the fixing altogether. Make sure you turn the base of the box either flat or slightly concave so that the box will be stable when finished.

Sanding and polishing the base

Sand and polish the base before removing it from the lathe. When sanding across the face of the box you will probably notice a small dot appearing in the centre. This is caused by a lack of surface speed on the wood in relation to the abrasive. At the edge of the box the wood is moving quite fast, but as you get nearer the middle, the surface speed slows down. The speed at the very centre of the box is effectively zero so no sanding is done. To get around this problem, stop the lathe after every other grit size and sand across the centre by hand, with the lathe stationary. The base can now be removed to allow the inside of the lid to be finished.

Finishing the lid

When you are sure you have finished using the lid as a friction chuck, take a single scraping from the side of the recess in the lid to ease the fit slightly. Ideally, the

Fig 6.8 *With the base held in the lid of the box and supported by the tailstock, light shearing cuts are used to round off the underside.*

Fig 6.9 *The finish on the lid can be improved by lightly shear scraping the surface. Note the hard edge left between the hollow and the edge of the recess.*

Fig 6.10 *The lid details should be turned using the spindle gouge in a shearing action to leave the best possible finish on the work.*

Fig 6.11 *Turning a small hollow in the lid will provide a point of interest on the finished box.*

Fig 6.12 *If a wooden friction chuck is made, a hole through the centre will aid the removal of the lid should it become stuck. Note the small sizing step in the end.*

lid should be a close but not tight fit on the base. Using the ³⁄₈in (10mm) spindle gouge, finish hollowing the lid to give a thickness in the top of about ³⁄₁₆in (5mm). This should then leave a step approximately ¹⁄₈in (3mm) wide at the edge of the recess. Refine the surface by shear scraping as before, to leave a hard join between the hollow and the recess to give a crisp appearance (see Fig 6.9).

Now turn the outer profile of the lid to produce a small, convex radius on the edge, working towards the recess (see Fig 6.10). On the outer diameter adjacent to this radius, turn a small concave surface about ³⁄₁₆in (5mm) wide and a mere ¹⁄₃₂in (1mm) deep. This small hollow will cast a shadow on the box and this will accentuate the lid details (see Fig 6.11). Sand and polish the lid before removing it from the lathe.

The top face of the lid can now be finish turned. Depending on what size you turned the recess, you may be fortunate and find that the lid can be lightly held directly onto the expanding jaws. If this is not the case, a friction chuck, as described in Chapter 19 (see Fig 19.5), can be turned into a length of scrap wood and the lid can be held on this using the tailstock for support as before (see Fig 6.12).

Taking light cuts only and starting from the edge, work in a slightly concave direction and blend this into a gentle convex surface as you progress towards the centre. Continue this until the edge of the lid has a hard, crisp corner meeting the small, concave groove in the outer diameter turned earlier. Finally, sand the

top surface of the lid. Take care not to soften the detail on the corners and be aware of heat building up on the surface as you will be sanding end-grained timber and heat shakes are likely. Polish and wax the lid before removing it from the lathe.

Fig 6.13 *The finished box, polished and waxed.*

Next steps

The basic techniques described in this chapter can be applied to many different styles of box – taller, fatter, the choice is yours. Texture can be added to the design by carving into the surface, or setting an inlay into the lid. Just turn away the wood and see what develops.

7 square
DESK BOX

**Kingwood. Height: 2in (51mm).
Width: 3in (76mm).**

F YOU HAVE COMPLETED THE PROJECTS in Chapters 5 and 6 you should find this square box relatively straightforward. Most of the methods used are a combination of the two previous projects. The square box is probably the most functional of all the pots and boxes that I make due to its stability.

As you have created one pot with square edges, you may wish to vary this design and remove the corners of the square blank to give an octagonal box. If you are new to square-edged turning, you will find this variation a little easier. After cutting the square blank to length, mark a circle on one end, then mark the 45° faces tangential to this. Set the mitre guide on the bandsaw to 45° so that the corners can then be removed. For longer blanks it is preferable to tilt the saw table instead. Be sure to hold the wood firmly against the guide or the edges will not be cut evenly. When you have removed three of the faces you will find there is very little wood in contact with the mitre guide and you must take extreme caution to ensure that your fingers do not slip (see Fig 7.1). The blank may be clamped for added safety.

Roughing out

Cut a blank 2¼in (57mm) long from 2½in–3in (64–76mm) square stock. With the blank between

Fig 7.1 *When using the bandsaw to remove the corners, extreme caution must be taken to ensure that your fingers are kept clear of the blade.*

Fig 7.2 *Turn a dovetailed step using the parting tool with the blade held over to the right by 15° and the handle to the left.*

centres, rough out the basic profile of the box. Turn a step in the top end to within ³⁄₈in (10mm) of the base of the box, with a diameter about ¹⁄₄in (6mm) less than the original size of the square. This step should be turned so that a sweeping curve is left between the square-edged base and the newly formed diameter. As with the square pot in Chapter 5, care must be taken not to splinter the edges.

At a point ¹⁄₂in (13mm) from the top face, turn a recess ⁵⁄₁₆in (8mm) wide, using a ¹⁄₈in (3mm) parting tool. Unlike the domed box, you need only turn the recess to a depth of ³⁄₁₆in (5mm) as the edges either side will not be rounded over.

Still using the parting tool, turn a dovetail mounting into the top of the lid, then undercut the square base until the diameter is equal to your chuck jaws. This should leave you with a step about ³⁄₁₆in (5mm) wide. Into this, turn a second, dovetailed step to suit your chuck (see Fig 7.2). Take care not to let the top of the blade touch the spinning edges or you will shatter the corners of the wood. Alternatively, as access is restricted, you may prefer to use a 15° form tool for this last step.

Using your thinnest parting tool, cut part way through the two halves, keeping to the right-hand side of the recess. Remember to leave a witness of the shoulder attached to the lid. Remove the box from the lathe and saw through the remaining wood on the bandsaw. If you use a narrow V block to support the work, as shown in Chapter 6 (see Fig 6.2), the square edge will be able to sit over the end of the support while the round section is safely cradled in the 'V'.

Now rough hollow the insides of the base and lid as described in Chapters 3 and 6 (see Figs 3.7–3.9 and Fig 6.3), before marking them with an identifying number and setting aside to fully dry and stabilize.

Refining the shape of the base

Once the timber has stabilized, remount the base of the box in the chuck. Refine the profile using the ³⁄₈in (10mm) spindle gouge. Starting at the top of the square corners, gently guide the tool down towards the shoulder of the box to produce a large, concave arc between the two. This should be turned until the thickness of the square edge is approximately ³⁄₁₆in (5mm) (see Fig 7.3).

Fig 7.3 *When turning the edges of the square, placing a card of contrasting colour in the background will help define the corners.*

Fig 7.4 *By holding the cloth pad well away from its end, your fingers will be better protected should the cloth catch. Note how the thumb of the left hand keeps the fingers tucked in.*

Now form the shoulder that will fit into the lid, using the end of a parting tool as described in Chapter 6 (see Fig 6.4). Ensure that the shoulder is turned parallel.

Move the tool rest across the bowl of the box to allow the inside to be finished to the desired thickness, using the spindle gouge as described in Chapter 3 (see Fig 3.9). If necessary, the surface can be further refined with a light shearing cut from a ½in (13mm) round-nose scraper.

Sanding and polishing the base

When sanding the box around the square edges, be sure to use both hands to hold the abrasive, as described in Chapter 5 (see Fig 5.9). This should help you avoid rounding over the edges or catching your fingers in the spinning corners. Remove the work from the chuck and hold a 2in (51mm) sanding disc in its place to sand over the square edges. When this is done, return the base of the box to the chuck and apply your chosen polish.

After the finish has dried and the wax has been applied, buff the surface to a low shine. For safety reasons, you should adopt a similar method for polishing as for sanding. Fold a sheet of soft, paper polishing cloth into a pad, and using both hands to give a firm grip, hold the pad at least ¾in (19mm) away from the end (see Fig 7.4). This way, if the cloth catches on the square corners your fingers will not end up covered in plasters. Remove the base from the chuck: the underside will be finished later.

Finishing the lid

Now remount the lid in the chuck jaws for finish turning. Using a square-ended scraper, turn in the shouldered recess as described in Chapter 3 (see Figs 3.11 and 3.12). At this stage, the recess should be turned so that the base of the box fits firmly as described in Chapter 6 (see Fig 6.7).

Mount the base in the lid of the box, using the lid as a friction chuck, and bring up the tailstock for added security. With the tool rest positioned across the base, as the tailstock will allow, finish turn the underside of the box. Using the ⅜in (10mm) spindle gouge, start at the edge and gently move the tool towards the middle, creating a slightly concave surface. Continue the cut until you are clear of the

Fig 7.5 *Using the lid as a friction chuck, the underside of the base is turned, first with a concave surface, then blending into a lightly domed middle area.*

Fig 7.6 *When blending the lid in with the base, care needs to be taken to avoid damaging the polished surface.*

square edges by about ¼in (6mm). Be sure to follow the profile on the upper surface of the base, or the square edges will end up with a tapered look. Once the outer area is completed, move on to remove the remaining wood from the centre of the base (see Fig 7.5). This should be turned to give a convex surface that will be about ⅛in (3mm) clear of the surface that the box is standing on when finished. For the last ⅜in (10mm) of the cut, you will need to remove the tailstock support, so great care must be taken not to exert too much force on the work in case you cause it to come loose.

Sand and polish the underside of the base but do not remove it from the lid just yet. Using the ⅜in (10mm) spindle gouge, turn the lower end of the lid down to the same diameter as the base, stopping short of the chuck jaws by at least ⅛in (3mm) (see Fig 7.6).

You must ensure that the gouge is held right over on its side to produce a fine shearing cut, and also to prevent the cutting edge from damaging the finished surface on the base of the box.

Remove the base and ease the fit of the two halves slightly by taking a light scraping from the diameter of the recess in the lid. The hollow in the lid can then be refined, using the spindle gouge followed by a light shear scraping.

Sand the lid to 400 grit before adding the final detail. Using the edge of a ⅛in (3mm) parting tool, cut a small shoulder into the corner of the lid, to a depth and width of ¹⁄₃₂in (1mm) (see Fig 7.7). This shoulder will give a definite visual break between the base and the lid of the finished box.

It should be turned after sanding as the shoulder would probably lose its crisp appearance if it were

Fig 7.7 *Finer details are often turned after sanding to ensure that the edges remain crisp.*

turned before. Finish the sanding and polish before removing it from the lathe.

Hold the lid on a wooden jam chuck and, for security, bring the tailstock up to support the lid. Turn the remainder of the outer diameter to blend with that turned earlier. Using fine shearing cuts, turn the top face of the lid to give a slightly concave hollow surface (see Fig 7.8). This will give a much better appearance than a plain, flat top. Now withdraw the tailstock: this will allow you to finish the centre.

Part sand the lid to 400 grit before turning a small step in the top corner to a depth of $\frac{1}{32}$in (1mm), to match the one in the underside of the lid. Carry out the final sanding and polishing before removing the lid from the jam chuck. You now have a finished box just the right size for those small secrets.

Fig 7.8 *With the lid held securely on a friction chuck, the top surface is turned with the edge of the spindle gouge to produce a slight hollow.*

Fig 7.9 *The finished kingwood box.*

8

globe pot
ON PEDESTAL

Osage orange and sonokeling. Diameter: 2⅞in (73mm). Length (tip to tip): 8in (203mm).

T HIS PROJECT WILL BRING TOGETHER all that you have learnt so far: turning fine finials, square-edged turning, hollowing etc. While this project is certainly more complicated than the previous four pots, it is not quite as daunting as it seems. If you break up the turning into individual stages – a central sphere, a pedestal and two finials – you will see that it is not that different from what you have already made.

In the previous four projects I explained the techniques used to create the various pots shown, along with the order in which the steps had to be carried out. For this globe pot I shall be concentrating almost entirely on the order of turning, so it will be helpful if you are familiar with the techniques required to make the previous pots and boxes.

Templates and gauges

One of the main ways in which this pot differs from the previous projects is that, if the globe is to be successful, a number of measurements must be taken at various stages of the work. This may be done using a combination of callipers, depth gauges and rulers. However, if you intend to make a number of the pots, it is far more efficient to make a template to gauge the work (see Fig 8.1). To help establish accurate

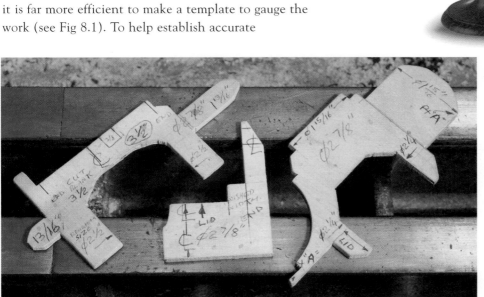

Fig 8.1 *The use of gauges can greatly speed up the time taken to measure the various dimensions.*

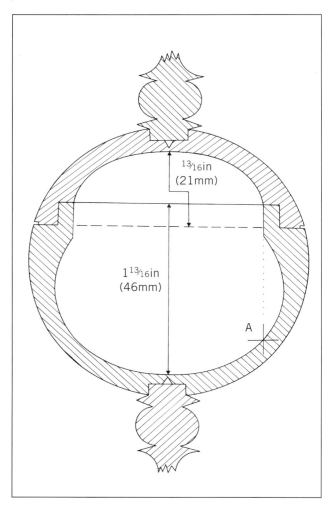

13/16in
(21mm)

1 13/16in
(46mm)

A

Fig 8.2 *This cross section, shown actual size, clearly illustrates the internal details of the globe.*

measurements, the sectional sketch in Fig 8.2 is drawn actual size so that dimensions can be transferred straight to the pot.

I suggest you make the central globe first as everything else is created to suit this. As the dimensions given in this project are relative to a globe with a finished diameter of 2⁷⁄₈in (73mm), you must ensure that the chosen timber is at least 3in (76mm) square, and cut a blank from this of no less than 3½in (89mm) in length. Although you will need to put the globe aside to stabilize after roughing out, it will help if the blank is fairly dry to start with, as excessive movement would make things difficult later.

Central globe

After roughing down to a diameter of no less than 3in (76mm), face off the ends to give a length of 3⁷⁄₁₆in (87mm). This will then leave you with ¹⁄₁₆in (1.5mm) all round to clean up later. The position of the centre line of the sphere and the shoulder for the lid can then be marked out from the left-hand edge at 1½in, 1⁷⁄₈in and 2¼in (38, 48 and 57mm).

Cut the lid fitting in to a diameter of 2½in (64mm) using a ³⁄₈in (10mm) beading and parting tool. Turn in a dovetail mounting ¹⁄₈in (3mm) wide at each end. Turn both to a diameter of about 2in (51mm) or to suit your chuck (see Fig 8.3). Remove some of the excess waste, in order to speed up the stabilizing process, by turning a 45° angle on each end

Fig 8.3 *A ³⁄₈in (10mm) parting tool is used to create the dovetail mountings at each end and to turn in the ³⁄₈in (10mm) wide recess.*

Fig 8.4 *The bowl is rough hollowed to 1¾in (44mm) in both depth and diameter, using the back hollowing method.*

to a width of ½in (13mm). Now cut partially through the two halves, to the right of the recess, using a fine-bladed parting tool and then cut through the remainder using a saw.

Remount the base in the chuck and rough hollow the inside, using a ⅜in (10mm) spindle gouge, to a depth of no more than 1¾in (44mm). Place a piece of adhesive tape on the gouge, 1¾in (44mm) from the end, to act as a depth gauge when boring the initial depth hole. Open up the diameter to no more than 1¾in (44mm), leaving a full radius in the bottom of the bowl (see Fig 8.4). Replace the lid in the chuck, rough hollow to a depth of no more than ¾in (19mm)

and open up to a diameter of no more than 1¾in (44mm). When this is done, put the two halves aside to stabilize and finish seasoning.

Finishing

After the wood has had a chance to stabilize, true up the top face of the base. Turn the shoulder for the lid fitting to a diameter of 2¼in (57mm), then finish to a width of ¼in (6mm) (see Fig 8.5). As the wood is fairly coarse and the surface area of the shoulder is quite large, refine the finish with a light shearing cut from a spindle gouge. Remember to keep the shoulder square and parallel.

Fig 8.5 *Using a ⅛in (3mm) parting tool, turn the shoulder for the lid fitting down to a diameter of 2¼in (57mm).*

69

Fig 8.6 *The inside is opened out to a diameter of 1¹⁵⁄₁₆in (49mm).*

Now turn the inside of the base to size to give a finished wall thickness of about ³⁄₁₆in (5mm). As the outside has not yet been turned to size, measure carefully to ensure that the inside will be an even thickness once the outer profile has been turned. Firstly, open out the bowl to a diameter of 1¹⁵⁄₁₆in (49mm) (see Fig 8.6). When this is done, finish the base of the bowl to a depth of 1¹³⁄₁₆in (46mm). This will then leave the base section slightly thicker than the rest of the wall to allow for the ³⁄₈in (10mm) hole which will be drilled later.

To help gauge the required curvature of the inside, a known position halfway around the radius needs to be created (see A on Fig 8.2). Using a straight-sided, single-point tool – I used the 15° Mole – enter it into the work to a depth of 1⁷⁄₁₆in (36mm) (see Fig 8.7). Slowly bring the tool out to the side until the edge just touches the 1¹⁵⁄₁₆in (49mm) diameter. The result will be a small step in the lower part of the bowl which can then be used as the point at which to aim when turning the inner radius.

Next, mark a pencil line inside the bowl at a depth of ³⁄₈in (10mm) from the top edge. Now you have established three known positions around the inside it is just a matter of joining them together, using the ³⁄₈in (10mm) spindle gouge in a scraping action. If necessary, the curvature can be checked using the end of a profile gauge. The surface finish can then be refined with a light pass from a ¹⁄₂in (13mm) round-nosed scraper before final sanding and polishing of the

areas turned so far. Remove the base from the chuck, to be finished later.

With the lid now secured in the chuck, turn the mating face true with the spindle gouge. Hollow the lid to a depth of ¹³⁄₁₆in (21mm), and open it out to a diameter of 1¹⁵⁄₁₆in (49mm). Using a square-ended scraper, create the recess that will fit over the

Fig 8.7 *A piece of adhesive tape placed at the correct position on the tool will act as a depth gauge.*

Fig 8.8 *The ⁷⁄₁₆in (11mm) square step will be used as an aiming point when turning the radius.*

shoulder of the base. The recess should be turned to a good push fit at this stage, as the base will be held in the lid while turning the outer profile.

Fix the base firmly in the lid and bring the tailstock up for added security. To turn the finished spherical profile, first reduce the cylinder to the finished size of 2⁷⁄₈in (73mm) diameter. Face off the end to a length exactly 1¹³⁄₁₆in (46mm) from the join of the two halves. Pencil in a centre line ³⁄₈in (10mm) from the join of the two halves and, using a parting tool, turn a step into the corner of the base ⁷⁄₁₆in

(11mm) wide and ⁷⁄₁₆in (11mm) deep (see Fig 8.8). This step will be used as an aiming point when turning the radius of the base, along with the centre line pencilled in earlier.

Now turn the spherical form using the spindle gouge. Start by removing the corner at 45° until you are within ¹⁄₁₆in (1.5mm) of the aiming point. You can then create the radius, working from the centre line, past the aiming point and down towards the tailstock (see Fig 8.9). As you begin to get close to the finished size check the profile, using a radius gauge, to ensure

Fig 8.9 *The radius is turned working from the centre line, past the aiming point and down towards the tailstock.*

Fig 8.10 *The curvature should be checked periodically to ensure that the form is not oval.*

that the form is spherical (see Fig 8.10). If the form is made even slightly oval, the globe will rock when placed on its stand. Once the lower profile is completed, partially turn some of the lid area in much the same way, stopping short of the chuck jaws by at least ³⁄₁₆in (5mm) for safety.

A hole must now be drilled in the base to a depth of no more than ¹⁄₈in (3mm). For this I used a ³⁄₈in (10mm) saw-toothed bit (see Fig 8.11). Select a low speed when drilling as the hole must be machined accurately to take the finial later.

With the lower half complete, sand and polish the base before removing it from the jam chuck. Now ease the fit of the lid slightly before sanding it to 400 grit. After this initial sanding, cut a small step, ¹⁄₁₆in (1.5mm) wide, into the corner of the lid using a parting tool. If this step is cut before the initial sanding, the edge would be softened too much. With the step cut, the lid can be finish sanded and polished before being removed from the lathe.

To finish the top of the lid, turn a spigot into a piece of scrap wood to suit the recess in the lid. With

Fig 8.11 *A ³⁄₈in (10mm) saw-toothed bit is used at a low speed to ensure that an accurate hole is made. Note the depth line that is marked on the side of the drill.*

Fig 8.12 *With the lid fitted to a jam chuck, the profile can be finished with the spindle gouge.*

the lid fitted to the jam chuck and the tailstock brought up for safety, finish the top end of the lid with the spindle gouge (see Fig 8.12), again checking the profile with the radius gauge. Finally, drill a ⅜in (10mm) hole to a depth of ⅛in (3mm), before sanding and polishing.

Finials

Prepare two blanks ¾in (19mm) square and 3in (64mm) long. I used sonokeling for the finials as it contrasts well with the Osage orange sphere. With small-sectioned dry or part-seasoned exotic wood such as this, there is normally no need to rough turn the work as there is little chance of it moving.

As the blank is of small section, it can be held directly in a set of small dovetailed jaws without creating a dovetail on one end first. With the tailstock supporting the end of the work, reduce the blank to a cylinder with a diameter of ⅝in (16mm). The first step is to turn a ⅜in (10mm) diameter spigot on the end to suit the hole in the globe. The length of the spigot should be made slightly less than the depth of the hole in the globe to ensure that the two pieces fit accurately. As I tend to turn rather a lot of ⅜in (10mm) spigots on different items, I have made a gauge that is permanently set at ⅜in (10mm). This is simply made from two pieces of square-section steel clamped to the sides of a length of ⅜in (10mm) square-section bar (see Fig 8.13). Alternatively, the spigot can be checked with callipers and then double-checked for size in the prepared hole before continuing.

Fig 8.13 *The ⅜in (10mm) spigot must be accurately turned so that it fits into the mating hole of the sphere.*

As an alternative to holding the finials in the dovetailed jaws, a small, ⁵⁄₁₆in (8mm) mini drive may be used. The tip of the finial is then supported with a hollow ring centre, while the head of the drive is small enough to be clear of the work when the ³⁄₈in (10mm) spigot is turned on the other end (see Fig 8.14).

Once the spigot is formed turn in the details, starting with the 'V' forms which are necessary to give a definite visual break in the profile between the globe and the finial. Turn the bead details next, then the hollows and so on, working gradually towards the tip of the finial. It is important that you are happy with each

stage before continuing, as once you reach the tip of the finial there will not be enough strength in the wood to support any further cutting at the base end. At the tip of the finial turn a small hollow so that the end of the hollow is slightly larger in diameter than the centre. This will leave a small head at the end of the finial when finished. The finished piece should now be about 2½in (64mm) in length.

Sand and polish the details before parting off with the long point of the skew chisel. This should be done to leave a slightly convex tip at the end. When separating the finial, you must support the work with

Fig 8.14 *The detail is turned in using a ³⁄₈in (10mm) spindle gouge. Note the ⁵⁄₁₆in (8mm) light-pull drive and hollow-ring centre which may be used if small dovetailed jaws are not available.*

Fig 8.15 *The tip is turned using the long point of the skew chisel to leave a slightly rounded end as the work is parted off.*

Fig 8.16 *Check that the globe fits neatly into the hollow of the pedestal.*

one hand while holding the skew chisel in the other, so take care not to catch your arm on the rotating chuck (see Fig 8.15). The tip of the finial can now be finish sanded by hand.

Pedestal

Prepare a blank 1⅝in (41mm) square and 3in (76mm) in length from the same timber that you used for the finials. The pedestal should end up being turned to a height equal to the length of the finials. In one end of the blank saw out a step ¼in (6mm) deep and at least ¾in (19mm) along the length of the blank. Repeat this on all four sides until you are left with a central square of just over 1in (25mm) across.

With the blank between centres rough turn the profile, keeping clear of the 1in (25mm) square end by at least ½in (13mm), and then create a dovetail on the lower end to suit your chuck. With the work now held directly in the chuck jaws, create a shallow hollow in the top of the square. Using a spindle gouge, start the cut at the edge of the square and work towards the centre, cutting against the grain, to a depth of about ⅛in (3mm). Check the globe in the hollow and adjust the curvature until both parts fit neatly together (see Fig 8.16).

Now turn the underside of the square support parallel to the top to give an even edge of about ³⁄₃₂in (2mm) in thickness. It is important, when cutting into an uneven edge, that the bevel is perfectly aligned with the direction of the cut before

the gouge is allowed to touch the work. Using a background of a contrasting colour will often help define the edges of the spinning square and help you to see the edge of the work. After you have turned the hollow in the end of the square section and the upper part of the stem, the square top and its edges need to be sanded before any further turning is done (see Fig 8.17).

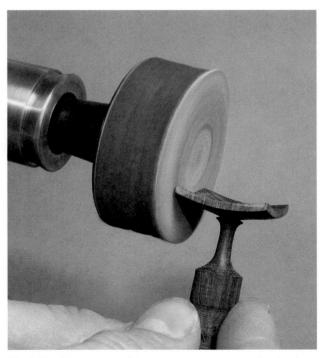

Fig 8.17 *The edges of the square support are kept crisp by using a 2in (51mm) disc sander held in the lathe.*

Fig 8.18 *The stem details are turned with the ⅜in (10mm) spindle gouge. Note how the contrasting background helps define the square edge.*

Next, turn a round bead into the centre of the pedestal using a fluted bead forming tool. This is an important part of the design as the rounded form of the bead links in with the spherical globe and helps to unite the separate parts.

Now turn the lower end of the pedestal, using the ⅜in (10mm) spindle gouge to create the final details before sanding and polishing (see Fig 8.18). Sand the underside after parting off the pedestal, using a 2in (51mm) disc sander held in the lathe.

With each part finished, glue the two finials into place. To ensure a good finish, make sure that you set the grain alignment of the finials in the same direction as that of the central sphere. You should now have a well-balanced globe pot sitting on a rather elegant pedestal.

Fig 8.19 *The finished pot in Osage orange.*

GALLERY

This collection illustrates various designs that could be made using the techniques covered in the previous chapters. Some of these follow closely the layout of the projects described, for others I have used a combination of the projects to create more varied designs. Feel free to copy them to begin with for practice, but do go back and see how you could vary the pieces. By altering the designs to suit your own particular style, you will soon open up many more possibilities for creating different shapes. I have included some dimensions but these should be treated as approximate only.

African ebony. Diameter: 2⅛in (54mm).
Using a dark timber with little or no figure, such as this African ebony, is very useful when testing a new design as it will allow you to see the silhouette and study the form more clearly. This design, with its captive ring on the finial, works particularly well as the tapered diameter at the top of the foot appears to carry through to the diameter at the base of the finial.

From left: Papua New Guinean ebony, pink gidgee, Rio rosewood. Diameter of largest piece: 2in (51mm).
With these more highly figured woods, did you notice the shape of the designs first, or the interesting grain patterns? While colourful timber can enhance a good design, it is important that you do not use interesting woods to try and hide poor work.

Cocobolo. Diameter: 2in (51mm).

Although these pots have a slightly more intricate design, the sudden changes of direction in profile help to emphasize the bold grain pattern of the wood.

Lignum vitae. Diameter: 2in (51mm).

The contrasting colours of heartwood and sapwood can often be used to enhance a design.

Bocote (Mexican rosewood). Diameter: 2in (51mm).

Notice how the bead detail on the finial is balanced by the small bead at the top of the stem.

Kingwood. Height of tallest piece: 5in (127mm).
The pot on the left is the least successful as the stem immediately below the top bead thickens out too quickly in relation to the top of the finial.

Zebrano. Diameter: 2¼in (57mm).
The dramatic striping of the zebrano works well when used on a detailed pot, but care should be taken when using such a bold figure, that the stripes do not conflict too heavily with the shape of the work.

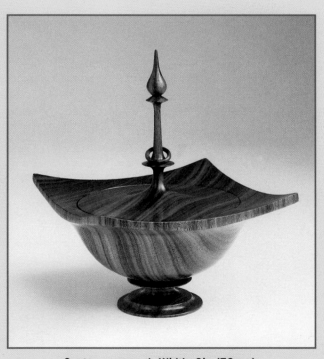

Santos rosewood. Width: 3in (76mm).
The addition of a captive ring adds further interest to a relatively simple finial.

*A design is only as good as its worst feature.
By improving the areas that are not often seen
you raise the quality of the piece dramatically.*

*Attention to detail on the underside of the
foot is also important.*

Goncalo alves. Width: 3in (76mm).
*The large expanse of end grain on the top of the pot shows off the
gentle variation in the colour of the timber.*

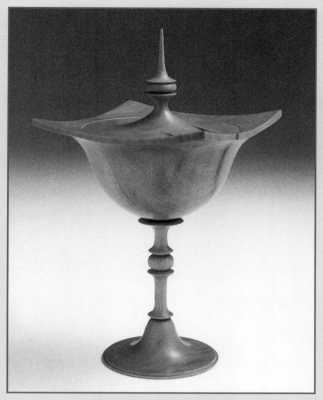

When adding decorative rings, consider turning a raised rim instead of just a shallow groove.

Pink ivory. Width: 3in (76mm).
The bead in the centre of the pedestal helps relate the design of the stem to the shape of the top finial.

From left: Bocote, kingwood, cocobolo, Papua New Guinean ebony and Osage orange. Largest width: 3in (76mm).
Notice how, by keeping the edges crisp, the details produce pleasing shadow lines. The two taller designs are less successful as the bases are too fat for the size of the pot.

Cocobolo. Width: 3in (76mm).
A slight taper towards the base of the finial will usually look more pleasing than a parallel stem.

Close-up of the foot detail.

Papua New Guinean ebony. Width: 3in (76mm).
Having such a wild figure can create an almost magical effect if the grain remains aligned when the lid is fitted. The addition of a square foot in the centre provides yet more variation.

From left: Tulipwood, cocobolo, kingwood. Width for all: 3in (76mm).
Hexagonal and octagonal pots – another variation. Notice how the eye is immediately drawn to the large area of pale sapwood on the centre pot.

From left: Tulipwood, snakewood, masur birch. Diameter of largest piece: 4in (102mm).
The tulipwood box was made with the grain running parallel to the vertical axis, whereas the snakewood and masur birch boxes were made with the grain running across the work to show their figure at its best.

Cocobolo. Diameter: 3in (76mm).
See how the small, and almost hidden, bead detail visually separates the lid from the base.

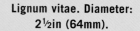

Lignum vitae. Diameter: 2½in (64mm).
By creating the box around the axis of the log a pleasing, and fairly even, colour contrast is achieved between the heart and sapwood.

Pink gidgee. Diameter: 3in (76mm).
A variation of the domed box, using harder edges. The small, raised bead detail on the lid provides a much needed reference at the change in direction.

Kingwood. Diameter: 2½in (64mm).
The changing curves on this box have a very pleasing effect on the figure.

Papua New Guinean ebony. Diameter: 3in (76mm).

While intricate designs can be fun, a simple shape will often be more successful in showing off highly figured woods. Notice how the sides of the box, and the face of the lid, have a slightly concave surface; this produces a far better effect than straight edges would.

The effect of the marbled figure is best seen on the end grain across the face of the lid.

Tulipwood. Width: 3in (76mm).

With a simple silhouette such as this, the proportions between lid and base are very noticeable.

Kingwood. Width: 3in (76mm).
The addition of a raised rim breaks up the flat surface of the lid.

A raised ring on the underside of the piece not only increases the appeal of the piece, it also helps to relate the design of the two halves.

View showing the full profile.

87

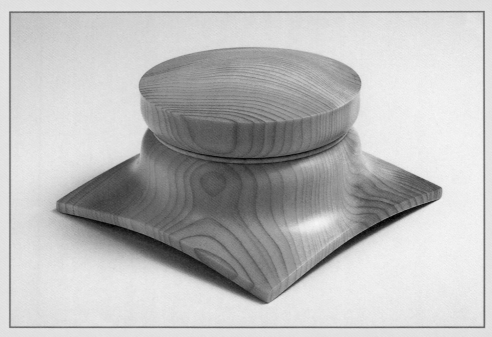

Yew. Width: 3in (76mm).
Combining the graceful curves of the domed box with the hard edges of the square desk box has a different effect on the figure.

From left: Tulipwood, pink ivory and kingwood. Height of tallest piece: 2in (51mm).
Notice how the small step in the top edge of the lid helps balance the effect of the join.

**Kingwood and tulipwood.
Diameter: 3in (76mm).**
The square base of the pedestal provides a pleasing contrast to the very rounded effect of the rest of the design.

**Tulipwood and African ebony.
Diameter: 3in (76mm).**
The brightness of the tulipwood sphere provides a stark contrast with the blackness of the African ebony finials.

**Rippled pink ivory and African ebony.
Diameter: 3in (76mm).**
The use of the rounded bead details in the centre of the pedestal and the finials relates both to the central sphere.

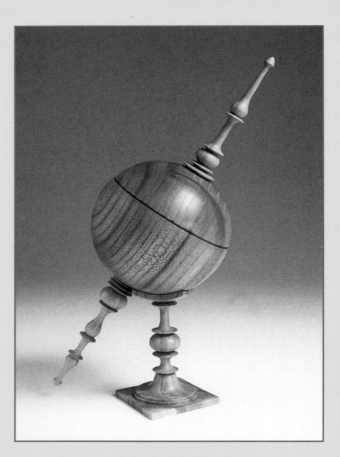

Wych elm and plum.
Diameter: 3in (76mm).
The combination of the wych elm sphere and plum finials gives a subtle combination of colours.

From left: Papua New Guinean ebony and snakewood, yew and Rio rosewood, ovankol and tulipwood. All diameters: 3in (76mm).
Notice how the small recess at the join of the two halves helps disguise the slight mismatch in grain around the burred area of the yew sphere.

PART THREE

Bowls

9 in preparation

I HAVE OFTEN FELT THAT ONE OF the greatest challenges to any woodturner must be the humble bowl, a category in which I include platters, dishes, open vases or whatever you wish to call the container. An unusual statement perhaps, but when you consider that man has been making bowls for thousands of years, the challenge is not just in the technical difficulty; it lies in the creation of an aesthetically pleasing design that is stimulating, functional (if necessary), and original (if possible). While it is perfectly natural to be influenced by what you see, try and vary the designs slightly. By varying and experimenting with designs, they will evolve naturally, and eventually you will add your own personal signature to the work.

Design

If you are designing a bowl that will be free standing and used to hold something, then a bowl with a small foot will not be the most ideal shape: a more stable design is needed (see Figs 9.1–9.4). Equally, if you are commissioned to make a piece that is to be displayed on a shelf 5ft (1.5m) from the ground, a flat design will be far from perfect. In this case a taller piece is called for or it will not be seen to its full advantage.

The design of the bowl may affect the way in which the bowl is mounted in the lathe and vice versa. If the work is going to be held by means of a dovetailed foot or recess, is this going to be incorporated in the design or removed at a later stage? If the bowl is going to be of a mainly practical nature, I usually try to incorporate the method of fixing into the design.

As with anything you make in wood, when you choose to make a bowl, the first thing you should do is study the material. Many bowls fall short of success purely because not enough thought has gone into positioning the bowl in relation to the figure of the wood (see Fig 2.21, page 22). If you wish to make a tall, open bowl but the timber would be better suited to a flatter, more closed design, don't fight it, select another piece of timber. If the bowl is to be wet turned then you must study the wood to see how the bowl will react as it dries out. There is little or no point in having a wavy bowl if it has twisted so far to one side that it will not stand up.

The design and form of a bowl is very much a matter of personal preference, though sometimes constrained by its intended function. Some people are drawn to very stable designs (see Fig 9.2) or to large, chunky bowls that use size for visual impact (see Fig 9.5). Others may prefer thin-walled bowls with small bases (see Fig 9.1). Whichever style you prefer, try to keep to soft flowing lines rather than lots of sudden changes in direction which will not be as pleasing to look at.

When judging the form of a bowl it is easy to be distracted by the markings in the wood, particularly in highly figured timbers. To overcome this, I study the form of the work not only when stationary, but also while the bowl is spinning in the lathe. This gives a better idea of how the finished piece will look. Also, when taking the final finishing cuts, I often watch the upper edge, or silhouette of the bowl as it is spinning, as I find it easier to judge the profile in this way. However, unless you feel confident with the gouge, I suggest that you watch the tool for the time being.

Timber

The choice of timber suitable for bowl work is vast, restricted only by your level of proficiency, but to begin with I suggest that you keep to native timbers such as ash or sycamore which are particularly easy to work. With the infinite number of design possibilities available within bowl turning, you will soon be able to show off the best in any timber, and the wood should show off the best in your work.

Practice

In the next few chapters I shall describe the methods used to make three different bowls. Working through these different designs will provide you with an

Fig 9.1 *Mulberry burr. Diameter: 3¾in (95mm). The form of this natural-edged bowl is pleasing but the small foot makes it impractical for use as a functional piece.*

opportunity to hone your skills on almost all of the bowl turning techniques you will ever need.

Finishing cuts

The use of fine finishing cuts is common to all the bowls. Therefore, I suggest that you take a little time to practise on some waste wood before proceeding with the following projects. For these cuts the bowl gouge is presented to the work with the cutting edge at a very acute angle – normally about 10° from vertical. When using the gouge at such a fine angle with the flute uppermost, there is always a risk that the tool will catch, as the upper wing of the tool is only a few thousandths of an inch from the surface. If this top corner of the tool comes into contact with the wood when you don't expect it, especially if you are turning the irregular rim of a natural-edged bowl, then a dig-in is likely.

You can greatly reduce the risk of this happening by using the gouge with the flute rotated away from the surface of the wood (anticlockwise if turning the profile on the inboard side of the lathe) by about

Fig 9.2 *Laburnum. Diameter: 14in (356mm). This large bowl has a far more functional shape.*

Fig 9.3 (profile of Fig 9.2)
A rare piece, as laburnum seldom grows to this size.

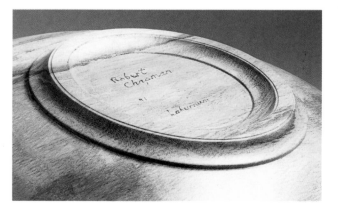

Fig 9.4 (base of Fig 9.2)
The large rim of the bowl's base provides a very stable design.

Fig 9.5 *The appeal of this yew bowl is its simplicity and the sheer mass of wood left in the thickness of the walls.*

160°, as shown in Fig 9.7. This will mean that you are using the gouge with the flute almost upside down, but if you look at the edge that is in contact with the wood, you will see that the relationship of the cutting edge is the same as if it were held with the flute uppermost. Holding the gouge in this way also causes the handle to be in a different position, often allowing it to clear any obstructions such as the foot of the bowl. Using the gouge in this way will not only produce a very fine shearing cut in a relatively safe way, it will also help you to use all the cutting edge on the gouge before it needs to be sharpened.

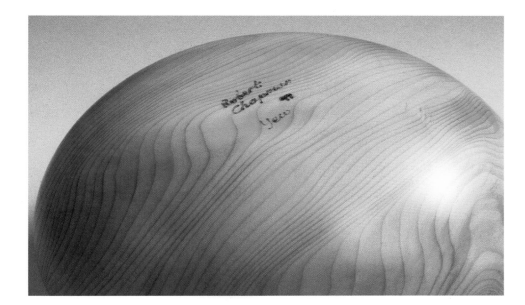

Fig 9.6 *The base has been finished off later as a dovetailed recess in a bowl of this style can often look clumsy.*

Fig 9.7 *By using the gouge with the flute upside down, a fine shearing cut is possible and the chance of a dig-in is greatly reduced.*

Fig 9.8 *If the gouge is not entered squarely to the diameter that is being cut, it may skate across the surface of the bowl.*

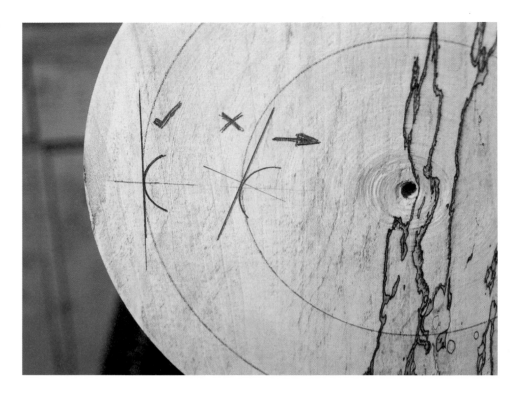

Tool control

As the gouge is entered into the wood, you should ensure that the curvature at the cutting edge is centred on the tangent of the diameter at the point at which you are cutting. If the gouge is entered with an incline to the right it will tend to skate towards the centre of the bowl (see Fig 9.8) and if it is inclined to the left it will try to pull out to the edge, which is even worse. If you are unsure about this, try the following simple exercise. Clean up the face of a blank and, with the lathe running at its lowest speed, touch the tip of a spindle gouge (with a fingernail grind) on the face of the work at the halfway point between the centre and the edge of the blank. Keep the handle of the gouge horizontal and the flute over to the right at 90°. While keeping the tool held lightly against the face of the wood, slowly rotate the gouge, first to the right and then to the left, and watch what happens. Note that when the gouge first makes contact with the wood, the bevel will not be in contact until the gouge actually penetrates the surface. Once this happens, the bevel of the gouge will have a positive surface to bare against and this will prevent it from skating out to the edge.

It is worth using the waste wood in the centre of bowls to practise with until you are confident enough to start the gouge in any position you choose. Mark a series of lines with a pencil, about $\frac{1}{4}$in (6mm) apart, across the face of the bowl and, using different size bowl gouges, practise entering the tool exactly on the line without it skating. After you have done this a few times, try it with a spindle gouge ground with a long bevel. Enter the gouge so that the bevel is in line with

Fig 9.9 *As the gouge is entered into the wood, the bevel must be kept in line with the direction of cut.*

the direction of the cut (90° for this exercise) and the flute is held over at 90° (see Fig 9.9). You should find the spindle gouge easier to start than the bowl gouge as the point of contact is smaller on the fingernail grind. Once you are familiar with this, practise starting the spindle gouge using one hand to hold the tool and just the thumb of your other hand to steady it. This practice will prove useful later when you are working close to the edge and need one hand to support the wall of the bowl as it gets thinner.

If you still experience difficulty in starting the cut in the bowl exactly where you want to, then use a parting tool to make a groove in the surface about 1/16in (1.5mm) deep to give the bevel of the bowl gouge an edge to locate on (see Fig 9.10).

Part turning

One final note; unless you wish to create a wet-turned bowl and retain the bark, or you specifically wish to have the bowl distort once it has dried (see Fig 9.11), each of the bowls shown will need to be part turned then put aside to be finished later when it is fully seasoned. This should be done even for dry timber as stresses released when removing the centre will cause the bowl to twist slightly. I am sure you will be keen

Fig 9.10 *Cutting a shallow groove with a parting tool will provide a shoulder for the gouge to rub on, preventing it from skating towards the edge of the bowl.*

to get on, but why not rough out a few extra pieces while you are preparing the blanks for the projects. This way, depending on their moisture content, these spare blanks will have stabilized by the time you have worked through the rest of the exercises.

Fig 9.11 *The edges on these oak bowls have twisted because they were turned green and allowed to dry after they were finished.*

10 nesting BOWL

Oak. Diameter: 8½in (216mm).
Depth: 1¼in (32mm).

THE NESTING BOWL IS VERY ELEGANT in its form; except for the inner rim, it is also one of the simplest bowls I make. For the novice, I suggest you leave out the inner rim until you have more experience. For the more advanced, this bowl can be made more complicated by adding further rims, though if this is overdone, the bowl will look too busy and complicated. With all form, simplicity is the key. I used oak for this piece but sycamore or maple are better for beginners as the grain of oak is quite coarse and can easily splinter when turned to a thin section.

Roughing out

Prepare a blank of about 8in (203mm) diameter and 1½in (38mm) thick.

Mount the work in the lathe on a screw chuck. A series of lines ground at intervals on the side of the drill bit will help you gauge the depth when drilling the hole for the screw.

Various types of screw are available, but my preference is for those made in stainless steel with a square-cut thread as they provide a more positive grip on the wood (see Fig 10.1).

Fig 10.1 *By using a parallel screw held in the chuck jaws, the length of thread can be adjusted without wooden washers.*

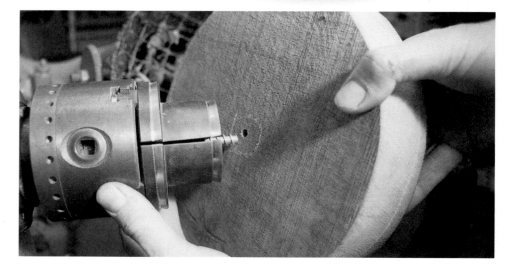

The lathe speed required for bowl turning depends very much on four main factors:

1 how large the blank is;
2 whether it has a high sapwood content or bark inclusion on one side causing imbalance;
3 the stability of the lathe; and
4 how experienced you are.

For efficiency I tend to select the highest speed the lathe, and the method of fixing, will cope with. However, while you are gaining experience, I suggest that you select a speed of no more than 1700rpm to begin with. With medium- and light-duty lathes, and also while you are learning technique, it would be wise to set yourself an upper limit of 1200rpm to preserve the life of your machine. If you are in any way uncertain, you should always err on the slow side and then increase the speed after some of the waste has been removed.

The first step is to turn away the bulk of the waste from the underside of the bowl. As my lathes are quite stable, I have no preference as to whether I true up the diameter of a narrow blank first or last. However, if your machine is fairly light or the blank is much thicker, then turning the rim first to remove any imbalance will help preserve the bearings. Using a ½in (13mm) bowl gouge held over on its side and with the flute facing the direction of cut, work from the centre out towards the edge. The gouge can either be pushed away from you across the work (see Fig 10.2), or pulled towards you (see Fig 10.3). The latter option is often easier if you don't have a swivel head and the bed of the lathe obstructs your access. Rough

Fig 10.2 *The underside of the blank is roughed out using the bowl gouge held on its side, pushing the cut from the centre towards the rim.*

out the profile using a series of cuts to produce the desired shape. While the finish is not that important at this stage, it is worth using the waste wood to practise with in order to build up your skills quickly.

Now turn a dovetailed foot in the base so that the bowl can be held in the chuck while you hollow the inside. For this I prefer to use a BCWA Mole as the angle of the cutting edge is ground at 15° to suit the chuck jaws. Alternatively, you could use a square-ended scraper reground to the same angle

Fig 10.3 *If you are working over the bed of the lathe, pulling the bowl gouge towards you will enable the handle to clear the lathe bed.*

Fig 10.4 *A 15° form tool is used to turn the dovetailed foot.*

(see Fig 10.4). Leave the diameter of the foot slightly larger than the intended finished size at this stage, as it will be turned again once the wood has seasoned. If you are using one of the collet chucks, I suggest that you create the dovetailed foot to suit one of the larger collets so that it can be reduced in size later on.

Remove the work from the screw chuck and remount it directly in the chuck jaws. I should point out at this stage that if you leave the bowl in the chuck overnight, or even just while you go for lunch, you should always check the jaws to see if they are still holding the bowl securely before you start the lathe. This is particularly important if the wood is unseasoned when you rough out as any shrinkage, which can occur quite quickly in wet wood, may cause the jaws to lose their grip.

Using the ½in (13mm) bowl gouge, rough out the inside of the bowl. Starting from the centre of the bowl, use the gouge with the flute on its side, facing the direction of cut. Remove the middle in a series of cuts working progressively deeper into the bowl, with each new cut starting nearer the rim (see Fig 10.5). Be sure to keep the bevel in contact with the wood at all times or tool control will be lost. With a shallow bowl like this, the gouge is entered into the wood at an angle of about 25° from the face of the work. This means there is little chance of the gouge trying to skate across the surface as the bevel makes contact with the work almost immediately and once this happens, you create a small shoulder in the work that prevents the tool from being influenced across the surface. On a deeper bowl, the gouge will often be

Fig 10.5 *The centre is turned away using the ½in (13mm) bowl gouge, working in towards the middle of the bowl.*

Fig 10.6 *A dovetailed recess is turned into the middle of the bowl, using a 15° form tool, so that the work can be remounted after seasoning.*

entered at a much steeper angle, sometimes as much as 90° to the face, so greater control of the tool is necessary (see Fig 9.8–9.10, pages 96 and 97).

Continue roughing out until the bowl is about ¾in (19mm) thick – more if the wood is particularly wet. Finally, turn a dovetailed recess in the middle of the bowl to suit your chuck jaws. This will enable the work to be remounted after seasoning (see Fig 10.6). Remember, when scraping the inside of a bowl, the tool should be cutting above the centre line, with the handle held higher than the tip rather than below, as it should be when you are working on the outside. Once you have reached the required thickness, set the work aside in a dry place until it has fully seasoned and stabilized or, if some movement is required, as in this piece, the work may be completed in one session.

Refining the shape

When the wood has stabilized, remount it in the lathe, holding on the recess that you turned inside the bowl earlier. Using a ⅜in (10mm) bowl gouge, true up the diameter of the bowl. Next, refine the surface by taking a light finishing cut using the side of the gouge at a near vertical angle to the wood to produce a very fine shearing cut (see Fig 10.7). It doesn't matter too much whether you use the gouge with its flute up or down at this stage, though generally it is safer to use it flute down while you are learning to gain control of it (see Fig 9.7, page 95). Stop the lathe and examine the surface closely for any torn areas that might benefit from further tool work before moving on.

Using the gouge with its flute up, and the cutting edge presented to the work at about 30° or 40° to

produce a levelling cut, turn the underside of the bowl true to remove any distortion that may have occurred during seasoning (see Fig 10.8). Using either the ⅜ or ¼in (10 or 6mm) bowl gouge, refine the surface finish further. Remember to keep the cutting edge nearly vertical to the surface of the work to produce fine shearing cuts (see Fig 10.9). During these finishing cuts it is important to cut the wood as cleanly as possible so that only a minimum of sanding is necessary. A little extra care now will save a lot of time during the sanding. It will help if you

Fig 10.7 *The rim of the bowl is turned using the side of the gouge to produce a shearing cut.*

Fig 10.8 *A levelling cut is taken with the gouge to finish shaping the underside of the bowl.*

can start the cut near the base and work towards the rim in one continuous, flowing movement. If the surface is cut in lots of small movements, the finished piece may end up rather lumpy until you master full control of the gouge.

Turn the base of the foot to produce a flat or slightly concave surface. If necessary, use a straight edge to ensure that the base is not convex. The diameter of the dovetailed foot can now be reduced to the correct size. Preferably, this should be of a size to

suit the form rather than the equipment in your workshop. However, if you are using a collet chuck this diameter will be determined by the collets you have available, unless the base is reverse turned later. Using a ¼in (6mm) spindle gouge with the sides ground right back (see Fig 10.10), turn the dovetail into the edge of the foot to blend in with the base of the bowl. Alternatively, a 15° form tool could be used for this as before, but once you have learnt good gouge control in tight spaces, a fine shearing cut from a gouge is always preferable for finishing.

To add decoration, cut a small bead into the surface of the foot using a ¼in (6mm) spindle gouge. Turn a small convex radius into the foot about ¼in (6mm) in from the edge. Repeat the cut the other

Fig 10.9 *A fine shearing cut will ensure that you don't have to spend excessive time sanding.*

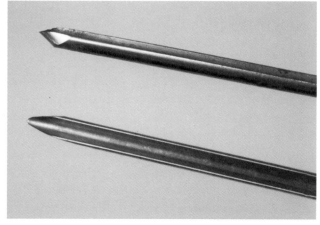

Fig 10.10 *The sides of these spindle gouges are ground right back to allow the tool to work in awkward areas. The bevel is also ground long to produce a fine finish.*

way, working out from the centre towards the first cut, stopping short of this by ¹⁄₃₂in (1mm). Where they meet you will be left with a small square ridge. Round this over using the tip of the gouge to produce a tiny bead. This adds interest to an otherwise plain looking base (see Fig 10.11). It is important to get a good finish on the bead to avoid ruining it by over-sanding, so I use a gouge with a long bevel angle to give a very fine surface finish.

Sanding the outside

Now sand the underside of the bowl and the rim. Start at about 80 grit and work down through the grades to around 400 or 600 grit, or finer still on dark exotic woods. For a small bowl such as this, with no details in the form, I have no real preference as to whether I use a power sanding disc or sand the work by hand with either a cloth- or paper-backed abrasive. The main rule is, as you sand near the edge of the rim, draw the abrasive out from the centre and past the rim of the bowl. If you work the other way around, or even worse to and fro, the crispness of the edge will be lost. For the same reason, sand the rim of the bowl working away from the headstock and out across the corner. Care must also be taken not to touch the edge of the foot with sanding discs: this area must be sanded by hand or the dovetail of the foot will be rounded over. The detail in the foot should also be carefully sanded by hand using the edge of the abrasive cloth. After sanding to 180 grit, stop the lathe and inspect the surface for any remaining torn

fibres. These must be removed by hand with the work stationary before you continue. There is no point in sanding a bowl down to 600 grit or more if you have not done the work properly with the 80 or 120 grit. With coarse woods such as this oak, it will help if the surface is sprayed with a mist of water to raise the grain prior to using the final grade of abrasive (see Fig 1.17, page 11).

After sanding, any dust left in the grain must be removed. The fastest, and by far the most effective way is to use compressed air to blow it out of the grain, but do remember to protect your eyes. If you do not have a compressor or air canister, a soft brush and tack cloth will remove some of the surface dust. Once the dust has been removed, give the outside of the bowl a liberal coating of sanding sealer, applied with a brush, and wipe the surplus off with a paper cloth. If you use a sealer which has been thinned down with 30% methylated spirit (50% for exotic timbers), you will find that it penetrates the wood far better than if you use it straight from the bottle. Note that the type of thinner required varies with different brands of sealer, so do read the label on the container first.

Once dry, the surface can be cut back with a fine 0000 wire wool or 1200 grit silicone carbide paper. The dust produced must be cleaned out again before a wax polish is applied. Beware when you are cutting back the sanding sealer as the dust produced can be quite harmful, often more so than the wood dust. The airborne particles of wire wool are not pleasant either, so use your dust extractor and wear a respirator.

Fig 10.11 *A small decorative bead turned with the tip of a ¹⁄₄in (6mm) spindle gouge will add interest to the underside of the foot.*

Fig 10.12 *Using a soft mop in the drill, the bowl can be polished much quicker than by hand.*

Buff the surface to a shine using a lamb's wool bonnet attached to the drill (see Fig 10.12). As well as being a faster method of polishing than by hand, this ensures that no lines are produced from dragging the cloth on the work too hard. Take care if you use this method of polishing on natural-edged work, or on bowls with bark inclusions, as the loose strands of wool will snag on the work. Finally, polish the foot with a hand-held cloth.

Finishing the inside

Hold the bowl with the dovetailed foot clamped in the chuck jaws. Place a piece of soft cloth over the foot before tightening the jaws to prevent them marking the wood.

True up the surface with the $\frac{3}{8}$in (10mm) bowl gouge to remove any distortion that has occurred. Reduce the thickness at the rim to approximately

$\frac{5}{16}$in (8mm) for a distance of about $1\frac{1}{2}$in (38mm). Further reduce this thickness to about $\frac{3}{16}$in (5mm), but this time for a distance of around 1in (25mm) only. This will become the outer rim of the bowl (see Fig 10.13). As the section becomes thinner, you will find it necessary to support the underside of the bowl lightly, using the fingers of your left hand, while controlling the tip of the gouge with your thumb.

Now it starts to get a little more difficult. The rim of the bowl needs to be further reduced, ideally to about $\frac{1}{16}$–$\frac{3}{32}$in (1.5–2mm) at the edge, to convey a light, delicate appearance when finished. If you are a little nervous about this, then leave the rim about $\frac{3}{16}$in (5mm) thick or more until you gain some experience. These final finishing cuts are easier if done with a $\frac{3}{8}$in (10mm) spindle gouge, ground with a fairly long bevel angle of about 60°. When starting a cut at the edge of a thin section, the gouge must be

Fig 10.13 *The outer step is turned down to $\frac{3}{16}$in (5mm) thick using the $\frac{3}{8}$in (10mm) bowl gouge.*

presented at the rim of the bowl so that the bevel is pointing exactly in the direction of cut and with the handle almost horizontal (see Fig 10.14). This will ensure that only the very tip of the gouge enters the wood to start with. Once the gouge has entered the wood, the handle can be lowered slightly as there will then be a surface for the bevel of the tool to bear against (see Fig 10.15). This will ensure that the cutting edge is shearing the wood to produce a clean finish. Note that the bowl should still be supported by your left hand to prevent the rim flexing away from the tool. Take fine cuts with each pass, gradually reducing the thickness. It is worth taking a little time to practise this technique when you are roughing out, rather than trying it out on a nearly finished bowl. If you are still a little nervous about reducing the edge in this way then use the method described next until you gain more confidence.

As the rim gets thinner there is very little margin for error. At this point it will help if the spindle gouge is brought into contact with the wood just inside the rim, with the flute facing out towards the edge of the bowl. Reduce the thickness gradually, pulling the gauge out towards the edge using the finest of shear scraping cuts (see Fig 10.16). This is working against the grain, but you will find it safer than working the other way. As the wood gets thinner it starts to vibrate, and if this happens when you are starting the cut at the rim you will shatter the edge. Once you have created a small step at the rim, you can revert to

Fig 10.14 *When reducing the width of the rim, the gouge must be presented with the bevel pointing exactly in the direction of cut.*

the usual method, working in towards the centre of the bowl for a distance of about 1¼in (32mm).

If you thought that was fun, cutting the small undercut for the inner rim is even better. This is done using a ¼in (6mm) spindle gouge with a long bevel and the sides ground right back (see Fig 10.10). Bring the gouge into contact with the outer rim you have

Fig 10.15 *Once the gouge has entered the wood the handle can be lowered so that the cutting edge is shearing the wood to produce a clean finish.*

Fig 10.16 *As the rim gets thinner it is easier to cut from inside the rim and work out to the edge, cutting against the grain.*

just cut so that the bevel is rubbing and the flute is rotated clockwise by 45°. Slowly move the tool into the base of the step for a short distance, creating a small undercut (see Fig 10.17). Next, enter the gouge from the top of the step, with the flute angled anticlockwise at 45° and the bevel in line with the intended direction of cut (see Fig 10.18). Turn away

the side of this step to blend in with the previous cut, then gradually turn away the two sides of the undercut step, working from alternate directions. Make sure you support the underside of the bowl with your fingers during this operation.

Before you proceed any further, the outer rim must be finish sanded. If it is left until later, the rim may

Fig 10.17 *With the bevel rubbing on the face of the outer rim, the gouge is slowly and gently eased forward to create the small undercut.*

Fig 10.18 *The bevel is lined up in the direction of the cut and the gouge carefully entered into the edge of the inner rim to turn down the side of the undercut.*

Fig 10.19 *When sanding under the edge of the rim it is important to keep your fingers at a safe distance from the sharp edges of the work.*

warp slightly, even if the wood is fully seasoned. If you try to sand it after it has distorted you will create an irregular thickness at the rim. Fold the abrasive cloth over to create a curved edge so that it can reach into the undercut of the inner rim. Hold the cloth, using two hands for stability, so that the curved edge is about ½in (13mm) from your fingers (see Fig 10.19). If you hold the cloth too near the edge, when you sand in the undercut you may cut your fingers on the inner rim. Remember to keep the abrasive moving so as not to create any ridges.

The inner part of the bowl can now be turned away using the ⅜in (10mm) bowl gouge. To produce a levelling cut, hold the tool on its side with the flute facing the direction of cut and the cutting edge at about 30° to the surface. Starting at the edge of the inner rim, reduce the first 2in (51mm) of the central bowl to about ¼in (6mm) in thickness (see Fig 10.20). Note that as the cut starts, the angle of entry will be quite steep (see Fig 10.21). This is necessary in order

Fig 10.20 *The ⅜in (10mm) bowl gouge is used for most of the final shaping inside the bowl.*

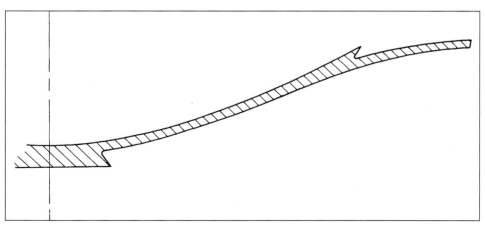

Fig 10.21 *This cross section of the bowl shows in detail the undercut of the inner rim.*

Fig 10.22 *When power sanding, it is safer to work only in the area between 9 o'clock and 6 o'clock. The edge of the inner bowl will become razor sharp after sanding and should be lightly sanded by hand to make it safe.*

the bowl much below ¼in (6mm) thick. On the outer rim I am quite happy to check the thickness with my fingers, but for the inner bowl I double-check with callipers: the thickness can be quite deceptive as you get nearer the base. Turn the bottom area of the bowl, working in small sections as before, and blending it into the surface already finished.

The inside of the bowl can now be finish sanded. For this I prefer to use a velcro-backed power sanding system to take the surface down to 400 grit before finishing by hand. To keep the inner rim crisp, sand from the inside working out to the edge. If you sand across the top of the rim, working in towards the middle, you will tend to round over the corner. When working through the final grades of abrasive, pay attention to where your hands and fingers are in relation to the edge of the inner rim. Due to the fine sanding, the rim will have developed a razor sharp edge (see Fig 10.22). This sharp edge should be lightly removed with 400 grit abrasive to gently soften it without removing its crisp appearance.

to reduce the thickness of the inner bowl to that of the outer rim. At this stage the edge of the inner rim will be quite sharp, so take care not to let your fingers come into contact with the spinning edge.

For the finishing cuts use a ¼in (6mm) bowl gouge – ⅜in (10mm) would suffice – and keep the cutting edge nearly vertical in relation to the path of the cut. Turn away the wood until you reach the desired thickness over the first 1½in (38mm) of the surface. By working small sections at a time, the wood left in the middle of the bowl is able to support the wood being cut. If the bowl is reduced in thickness evenly, all over, in one go, it would be very difficult to turn

Remove the dust from the surface before applying the sanding sealer. Be sure to use the same concentration of mixture as you used on the underside or slight colour variations may occur. When the sealer is dry, cut it back with 0000 wire wool and wax, before buffing to a shine with the lamb's wool bonnet. The outer rim should be polished with a hand-held cloth, but be sure to keep the cloth moving over the work. If the cloth is held in one place, fine lines can be produced as the wax will harden on the cloth and then scratch the surface of the work. Remember that the lighter you use the cloth or polishing mop, the higher the shine.

Fig 10.23 *The polished nesting bowl.*

11

traditional BOWL

Spalted sycamore. Diameter: 9¾in (248mm). Depth: 3in (76mm).

THIS DEEPER STYLE OF BOWL is probably the shape most commonly made by woodturners. It is elegant in its simplicity and functional due to the stability provided by its relatively large base. This base could be enlarged to provide greater stability if necessary. While I prefer the bowl to have a relatively fine wall, there is no shame in leaving the walls ½in (13mm) thick or more. Apart from being easier and quicker to make, the overall thickness and effect of a piece should be a matter of personal taste and not dictated to you by others.

Roughing out

After preparing a blank, about 8in (203mm) in diameter and 3in (76mm) thick is ideal to practise with, mount the work in the lathe on a screw chuck (see Fig 10.1, page 98). I find this method suitable for work up to about 12in (305mm) in diameter, but for larger, deep work I tend to use a 3½in (89mm) faceplate for extra security.

Using a ½in (13mm) bowl gouge held over on its side, with the flute facing the direction of cut, true up the diameter of the work. Next, turn away the bulk of the waste from the underside of the bowl, chamfering the corner of the work at 45° (see Fig 11.1). With the gouge still on its side, rough turn the profile of the bowl in a continuous curve, working from the base out to the rim of the bowl.

Fig 11.1 *The bulk of the waste is turned away from the underside at 45°.*

Fig 11.2 *The base must be finished either flat or concave when scraping the surface ready to glue on the scrap wood.*

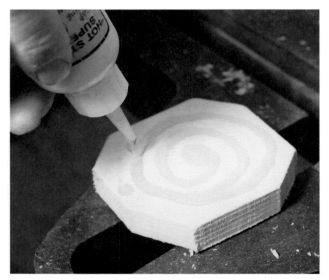

Fig 11.3 *A quick-setting glue is used to secure the waste block onto the foot of the bowl.*

Rough turn the foot of the bowl with the gouge before lightly scraping it flat to accept a glued scrap block. To do this, use a 1in (25mm) scraper with a slightly domed end. Ensure that the cutting edge is used trailing slightly downwards (see Fig 11.2). A few small grooves cut into this with a pointed scraper, or the corner of a parting tool, will help take up any excess glue. Check the foot for flatness with a straightedge before gluing on a piece of scrap wood. (This will be turned off later.) Blockboard or a good quality plywood are particularly well suited for this, but beware of cheap plywood as the layers can be forced apart when held in the jaws of a chuck. If you use a cyanoacrylate adhesive, such as Hot Stuff, with an accelerator, you will be able to turn the wood block almost immediately (see Fig 11.3). Once the glue has set, the block can be turned true.

Fig 11.4 *Using a 15° form tool, a dovetailed mounting is turned into the scrap wood.*

Fig 11.5 *A decorative dovetailed recess can be turned directly into the base if you don't wish to reverse turn the base off.*

Create a dovetailed foot using a 15° form tool, ready for remounting in the chuck jaws (see Fig 11.4).

If the wood still has a high moisture content and is liable to move a great deal during seasoning, I suggest that you turn an oversized dovetailed mounting directly onto the base of the work and glue on the block later when the wood has dried. The force of the movement in the wood while it is drying tends to separate the glue joint. This is particularly so in the case of wet, burred woods. Alternatively, if you do not wish to reverse turn the bowl, a dovetailed recess can be formed directly in the wood inside a footed base (see Fig 11.5). The latter method is particularly suited to larger work where reverse chucking would be impractical.

With the work now remounted in the chuck on the glued block, the inside of the bowl can be roughed out. If you feel you are not yet fully proficient in the use of the bowl gouge, instead of just roughing out the centre use this waste area to practise gouge control (see Figs 9.8–9.10, pages 96 and 97).

Starting from the middle of the bowl, with the flute of the gouge on its side, turn away a small hollow in the centre of the bowl. Continue turning away the centre of the bowl in stages, with each cut starting closer to the edge and going deeper into the blank, keeping the bevel rubbing at all times (see Fig 11.6). Repeat the cuts until the middle is roughed out to leave a wall thickness of about ⅞in (22mm) thick – more if the moisture content of the wood is fairly high.

Next, turn a dovetailed recess in the bottom of the bowl to enable the work to be remounted after seasoning. On a deep bowl such as this, you may not be able to hold on a recess cut in the base of the bowl, especially if you are using one of the collet chucks. If this is the case, when you are roughing out, leave a raised step of about 3½in (89mm) in diameter in the middle and turn the dovetailed mounting into this. When this is done, put the work aside to dry.

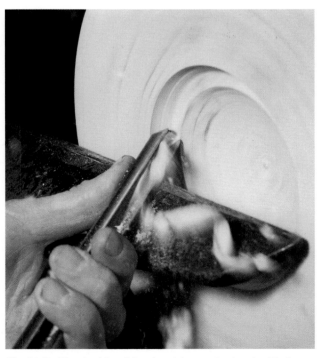

Fig 11.6 *The inside of the bowl is roughed out with the ½in (13mm) bowl gouge used on its side.*

Fig 11.7 *With the side of the gouge held at 25° to the surface, a levelling cut is taken to true up the outside after seasoning.*

Finishing the outside

Once it is dry, remount the bowl in the lathe, holding on the dovetailed recess inside the bowl. True up the outside and create the desired profile using a levelling cut from a ½in (13mm) bowl gouge (see Fig 11.7). Improve the surface finish with fine shearing cuts from either a ⅜ or ¼in (10 or 6mm) bowl gouge. The final cuts should be made with long, continuous movements, or the form may not be as pure as you would like.

If you are working spalted wood or any timber with an area of softer sapwood, you may find that you are left with a problem area where the fibres of the wood have torn out (see Fig 11.8). To remedy this, apply a generous coating of sanding sealer or finishing oil to the affected area then re-turn the surface, taking a fine cut with a ¼in (6mm) bowl gouge to remove the damaged area (see Fig 11.9).

Next, turn the detail of the foot using a ¼in (6mm) spindle gouge (see Fig 11.10). By keeping these details as crisp as possible, the foot will be far more elegant than if it were simply a raised bump at the bottom of the bowl. Remember to re-turn the dovetail in the scrap wood so that it runs true to the profile of the bowl.

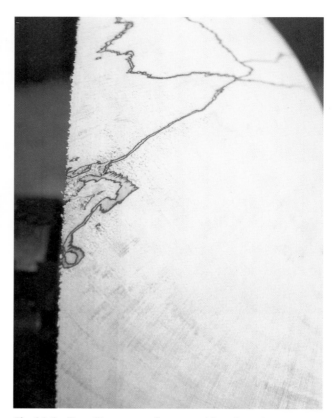

Fig 11.8 *Torn fibres are often a problem in soft or spalted woods.*

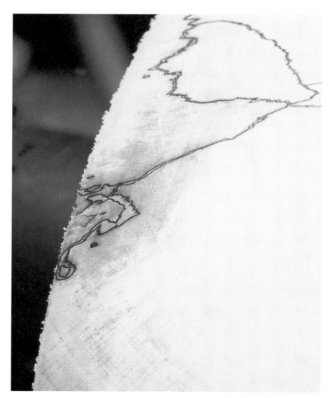

Fig 11.9 *To improve the surface finish, a coat of sanding sealer or finishing oil is applied to the affected area before taking a final shearing cut with the gouge.*

Fig 11.10 *A ¼in (6mm) spindle gouge is used to turn the fine details into the foot.*

Sanding the outside is relatively simple on a bowl such as this, so power sanding is used to smooth the upper area. The detail of the foot must be sanded by hand if you are to retain the crisp appearance. If you are working soft, spalted wood or one with a pronounced difference between winter and summer growth, such as ash, then care must be taken when power sanding: the surface can become uneven if there are hard and soft areas in the wood. For these timbers it is often better to sand the surface by hand. To do this, hold the abrasive firmly in both hands and brace them against your body to prevent the abrasive from following the contours of the hard and soft areas. Clean off the dust and brush the surface liberally with sanding sealer, wiping off the surplus with a soft paper cloth. Once the sealer is dry, it can be cut back with wire wool, waxed and buffed to a shine (see Fig 10.12, page 104).

Finishing the inside

Reverse the bowl in the lathe, holding the dovetailed base directly in the chuck jaws. Clean over the surface of the rim to remove any irregularity then refine the rim with light shearing cuts from a ⅜ or ¼in (10 or 6mm) bowl gouge (see Fig 11.11).

As the bowl is deeper than that in the previous chapter, position the tool rest at 30° inside the bowl to give maximum support to the tools. The inside of the bowl can now be finish turned. This should be done in stages, finishing a series of short areas at a time. The ⅜in (10mm) bowl gouge is used with the flute held over on its side to produce a levelling cut.

Fig 11.11 *The rim of the bowl should be turned to leave sharp corners as these will accentuate the shadows, giving a crisp appearance to the finished bowl.*

Fig 11.12 *The inside of the bowl is turned away in stages so that the remaining wood provides support for the cut.*

The cutting edge should be about 25° from vertical. Start by turning away the inside to about ½in (13mm) thick for a distance of 2½in (64mm) into the bowl (see Fig 11.12), then reduce the wall further to ¼in (6mm) thick, but this time for a distance of only 1¾in (44mm). The first 1½in (38mm) inside the bowl can then be turned down to its final thickness of about ⅛in (3mm). For the final shearing cuts at the edge of the rim, use either the ¼in (6mm) bowl gouge or the ⅜in (10mm) spindle gouge as described in Chapter 9 (see Fig 9.9, page 96). As the wall of the bowl becomes thinner, you will need to support it with your left hand to stop it from vibrating (see Fig 11.13).

This first step, and the rim, should now be rough sanded down to at least 240 grit before moving on. If the rim moves slightly and it is sanded later, the edge will become uneven. The sanding of subsequent steps can be left as these can usually be sanded safely later. The exception to this is if you are finishing a bowl from wet wood in one go. In this case, each section should be sanded as it is turned as the distortion will often be too great to allow sanding later.

Continue removing the rest of the inside in the same way, levelling short steps with the ⅜in (10mm) gouge, finishing with the ¼in (6mm) gouge, and blending them into the previously turned sections. Do not forget to check the thickness of each section as it is cut before you move on, as you may not be able to come back to it after the remaining wood, which provided support, has been turned away.

As you near the bottom of the bowl you may find that the ¼in (6mm) bowl gouge no longer has the rigidity to work so far over the rest. As soon as this becomes a problem you should start using the ⅜in (10mm) bowl gouge for the finishing cuts, ½in (13mm) on larger bowls, or the tool will chatter, producing an uneven surface (see Fig 11.14).

Fig 11.13 *You will need to support the wall of the bowl to stop it vibrating as it gets thinner. Notice how the bevel of the spindle gouge is in line with the start of the cut.*

Alternatively, an angled gouge can be used as described in Chapter 12 (see Fig 12.15).

Once the inside has been turned, finish sand the surface, working down through progressively finer grades of abrasive. I tend not to use power sanding on the inside of deeper bowls made of coarser woods such as elm and ash. The surface is so steeply concave, the sanding discs tend to remove more of the summer growth than the winter growth, producing a slightly rippled surface. This effect is made even worse if you use one of the soft-backed sanding discs. After you have finished sanding the inside, clean the surface and you are ready to seal and polish the work.

Finishing the underside

All that is left now is to reverse the bowl so that the scrap wood can be turned away and the underside of the foot can be decorated. There are a number of ways in which this can be done, some of which are described in detail in Chapter 19.

Fig 11.14 *By using the gouge right over on its side, the angle of approach is altered, reducing the distance the tool overhangs, yet retaining bevel contact.*

Fig 11.15 *The finished bowl in spalted sycamore.*

natural-edged BOWL

Field maple burr. Diameter (at top edge): 6in (152mm). Height: 5½in (140mm).

THE NATURAL-EDGED BOWL has always held a certain fascination for me, probably because nature plays such an important part in determining how the final silhouette will look.

Using various designs that have been tried and tested on regular flat- or smooth-rimmed bowls, you can gain a whole new effect by using the edge of a log to form the rim of the bowl. This is especially true in the case of burred woods, where the irregular edge gives a highly textured rim – even more so if the bark is kept on, as this contrasts with the colour of the wood itself (see Fig 12.1). Very often the bark separates from the log. This tends to happen when the log has dried out naturally, before the bowl is turned. If you can turn the wood while it is still green, you will stand a greater chance of retaining the bark, as the fungus that causes it to separate becomes inactive once the wood has dried out. So, contradicting my philosophy of part turning almost everything I make, this is the exception to the rule, but only if I am able to work the log when freshly cut.

Preparation

Once you have determined the position of the blank, cut this section from the log (see Fig 12.2). With the rough blank removed it can be further reduced, using the bandsaw to make it roughly circular, as described in Chapter 2 (see page 25).

With the blank cut, a method of mounting the work in the lathe is needed. For almost all natural-edged work I prefer to use the 1¼in (32mm) expanding pin jaws made by BCWA to hold the work. These expand into a pre-drilled hole (see Fig 12.3) and provide a firm grip on the timber, enabling the outside of the bowl to be turned (see Fig 12.4). Alternatively, you could use a conventional pin chuck to drive the blank, though with softer timbers or spalted woods the pin can sink into the wood and lose its grip. It's worth noting that when you drill the hole

Fig 12.1 *This masur birch bowl is made more interesting by the retention of the bark around the rim, which provides a pleasing contrast in colour.*

you do not have to drill straight down into the work, particularly if you are using a prepared blank from a timber stockist in which the top is angled to the rest of the blank. Instead, angle the drill so that the hole produced is square to the top face, using the opposite high and low points of the circumference as a

reference. This will ensure that the finished piece has a more balanced appearance.

Roughing out

Before starting work, check for any loose areas of bark that may fly off; these must be removed before the lathe is started. With the blank securely held on the pin jaws, you are ready to start turning. For larger blanks, those over 12in (305mm), I suggest using the tailstock for additional support until the blank is turned true. Select a suitable speed. This will depend very much on how irregular the blank is. In the case of a small bowl such as this, I tend to rough out the

Fig 12.3 *With the blank securely held, a 1¼in (32mm) hole is bored with a spade drill in the top of the work so that it can be mounted on the expanding pin jaws.*

Fig 12.4 *Expanding pin jaws provide the most effective way of mounting natural-edged bowls for roughing out.*

Fig 12.5 *By cutting from the top towards the base, the bark is supported by the wood underneath and is less likely to separate from the wood.*

work at between 1400 and 1800rpm increasing the speed once the work is balanced. However, if you are working on a light machine it would be wise, for safety, to select a fairly low speed to begin with.

The outer profile can now be rough turned, using the ½in (13mm) bowl gouge held over on its side. Starting at the base and working towards the headstock, turn the corner of the blank away at about 30°. Turn the diameter true in the same way.

When working over the natural-edged area, it is wise to cut from the top of the blank and work towards the base (see Fig 12.5). This method will ensure that the bark edge is supported by the wood beneath it. If you cut the other way when working with the grain, even if it is how you were shown in the past, the bark may be forced away from the bowl. Take care if you are using a conventional pin chuck or

you are only holding on a short distance of an expanding pin chuck. In such a case, be sure to bring up the tailstock when working towards the base of the work or the blank may be forced off the chuck.

The rest of the waste can be removed working with the grain, towards the headstock. Continue rough turning until you reach the profile you desire (see Fig 12.6). Do not turn away the foot to its finished size at this stage.

Turning the foot

For the foot of the bowl you have a choice. You can either create a dovetailed foot that will become part of the design (as for the Nesting Bowl in Chapter 10), or choose a plain-footed base as shown in Fig 12.1. In either case the foot should be left oversize at this stage. If there is enough surplus wood – ³⁄₈in (10mm)

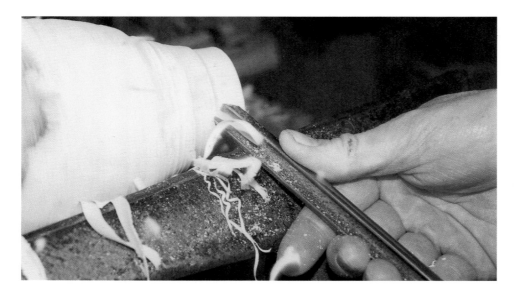

Fig 12.6 *The lower part of the bowl is roughed out using the ½in (13mm) bowl gouge, cutting with the grain and working towards the headstock.*

or more – left at the base of the work, a dovetailed foot can be turned directly into this. If not, glue on a piece of scrap wood as described in Chapter 11 (see Fig 11.3, page 110).

This foot will be used to hold the bowl while you hollow the inside, and then cut off later. It is helpful, though not essential, to leave the foot at least 2in (51mm) in diameter at this stage, to provide the necessary support while roughing out the inside. If you turn a foot that will remain as part of the design and work the outer profile to a finished state in one go, it will take a lot longer to hollow out the bowl. The small foot will lack strength at the base and you will

often be forced into taking smaller cuts or risk splitting the wood at the base.

Remove the work from the pin jaws and remount in the lathe using the larger 2½in (63mm) chuck jaws. Rough out the centre of the work using either the ½ or ⅜in (13 or 10mm) bowl gouge held over on its side, with the flute facing the direction of cut.

Start at the middle and gradually work down deeper into the bowl, starting each cut nearer the edge of the bowl as you progress deeper inwards (see Fig 12.7). Good gouge control is needed at this stage, with only small cuts being taken until the irregularity of the natural edge is removed from the centre.

Fig 12.7 *Small cuts are taken with the bowl gouge until the uneven edge of the bowl is removed.*

Fig 12.8 *Using a 15° form tool, a dovetailed recess is turned near the top of the rim. This will enable the bowl to be rechucked after seasoning.*

Fig 12.9 *The undercut beyond the inner dovetail mounting is clearly illustrated in this cross section through the bowl.*

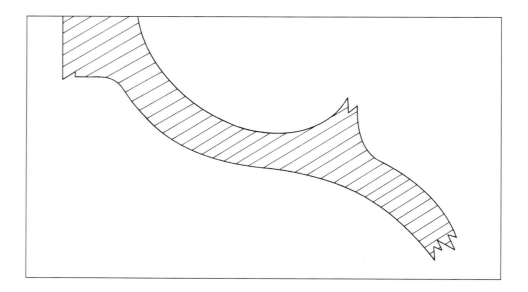

Continue until you are left with a wall thickness of about ⅝in (16mm), or ½in (13mm) if you are going to finish it while it is still green. Once you have removed the irregularity of the top surface you can take slightly larger cuts as you progress deeper into the bowl.

At this stage you should leave a step in the wall, increasing the thickness to about ⅞in (22mm) for a distance of ½in (13mm). Into this area turn a small dovetail recess. This will be used to hold the bowl after it has been rough turned (see Fig 12.8).

If you are using a collet chuck, leave the wall of a thickness that will allow your largest collet to fit the recess later (see Fig 12.9).

Now finish roughing out the lower area of the bowl to give a wall thickness the same as the rim.

This will give a slight undercut below the dovetailed recess, which will help keep a more even thickness in the work and also help prevent the work from splitting as a result of the wood drying too unevenly.

If you are going to finish the bowl while it is still green and allow it to move naturally afterwards, keep on reading. Alternatively, put the blank aside at this stage to finish seasoning.

Finishing the outside

To remount the work, secure the blank using the larger of the dovetails on the 2½in (63mm) chuck jaws (or large collet chuck) to grip into the inner recess that you cut earlier. If the blank has been part turned and then seasoned, true up the surface first and

Fig 12.10 *With the flute of the gouge nearly upside down, the cutting edge is kept at about 10° to the surface to produce a fine shearing cut.*

bring it back into round using a levelling cut. At this stage, remove any loose areas of bark or moss using a wire brush to lightly clean the surface.

Next, use either a ³⁄₈ or ¹⁄₄in (10 or 6mm) bowl gouge to take fine shearing cuts, working from the base up towards the edge of the bowl, cutting with the direction of the grain. During these finishing cuts, it is important to cut the wood as cleanly as possible so that a minimum of sanding is necessary. To obtain these finer cuts, present the cutting edge of the tool to the wood in as near a vertical position as possible.

If you are following the design shown here, which has a top edge that flares out, the bevel may not always be able to make contact with the wood while you are working around this upper part of the outer surface. You will find that the foot of the bowl often restricts the positioning of the handle. If this is the case, rotate the gouge anticlockwise: this will change the position of the handle relative to the cutting edge (see Fig 12.10). The cut can then be made with the flute almost upside down, as described in Chapter 9 (see Fig 9.7, page 95).

When taking the final finishing cuts near the top of the bowl, the cut will be intermittent. It is important at this stage to keep the gouge moving along in one continuous movement. If you try and finish the surface in several short movements, or stop the cut mid-way along, it can be more difficult to see where you left off due to the blurring effect of the

natural edge. If necessary, this effect can be minimized by placing a background of contrasting colour directly behind the work. This will help show up the irregular edges. Continue shaping the outside in this fashion until the desired profile is achieved, being careful not to damage the top edge of the bowl.

If you are going to create a dovetailed foot that will be part of the finished design, now is the time to turn it to size. If not, leave the lower area of the bowl slightly larger than the finished foot will be, to provide extra support when you work the inside. Return the dovetail at the base, or in the scrap wood, to ensure that it will run true to the bowl. Finally, if the bowl is to be reverse turned later to remove the foot, mark the centre point on the base to aid alignment later before going on to sand and polish the outside.

When sanding any natural-edged work, take care not to soften the crispness of the edge or the finished effect will be less appealing. If the bowl is fairly large, power sanding using a hard, foam-backed holder can help speed up the process. If you adopt this method, you must be sure to hold the drill firmly against your body, applying only the lightest pressure to the work. If this is not done, the sanding disc will remove a lot more wood from each leading edge as it spins round, creating a tapered effect on the edges. The effect is even worse if you use one of the softer varieties of foam-backed pads where the foam is on the abrasive disc rather than on the holder. To ensure that the

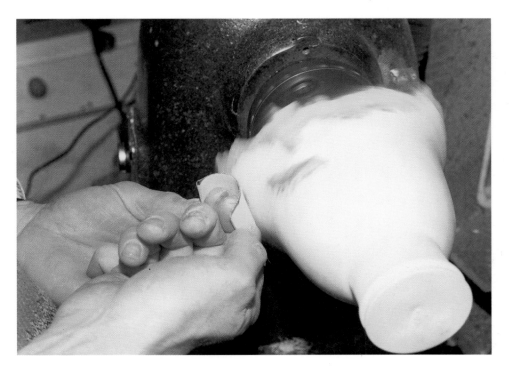

Fig 12.11 *Keeping both arms braced against your body for greater control, bring the abrasive into contact with the wood, using a minimum of pressure, to avoid softening the edges.*

edges remain crisp, I suggest that you sand the top edge of the bowl by hand. Hold the abrasive with both hands, stretch the cloth or paper between your fingers and keep your arms firmly against your body (see Fig 12.11). This way, if the cloth does catch, it should snatch from your hands without dragging your fingers into the work. Apply only a minimum of pressure to the work so that the crisp edges of the bowl remain intact and are not rounded over and softened. Draw the abrasive across the surface, rather than pulling it back and forth, working in one direction towards the headstock. Sanding in this way will also help retain the crispness of the edge. After sanding, clean and polish the surface before removing the bowl from the lathe.

Finishing the inside

Remount the work, gripping the dovetailed foot in the chuck jaws. Position the tool rest so that it is inside the bowl at an angle of about 45°: this will give maximum support for the tools. Using the ⅜in (10mm) bowl gouge, remove the bulk of the waste from around the rim to give about ¼in (6mm) in wall thickness (see Fig 12.12). Continue these cuts into the bowl to a depth of no more than 1½in (38mm), working in small areas at a time so that the wood being cut is supported by the waste left in the lower area of the bowl.

Change to the ¼in (6mm) gouge and reduce the surface further – down to ⅛in (3mm) thick. As for the outside, these final passes with the gouge should be as clean as possible to save on the amount of sanding later on. Present the cutting edge to the work at about 10° from vertical to ensure that a clean cut is achieved (see Fig 12.12). This can be done either with the flute uppermost, or with the tool upside down as described in Chapter 9 (see Fig 9.7, page 95).

Whenever the thickness is to be less than ¼in (6mm), the outside of the bowl should be lightly supported with the fingers of your left hand so that the wood does not vibrate. Supporting the bowl in this way will mean using just your thumb to guide the gouge, so some experience and good tool control is necessary (see Chapter 9, Figs 9.8 and 9.9). You must take care not to catch your hand on the spinning edges as you will be working perilously close to the uneven edge. If you are in any doubt over this stage it is best to err on the side of caution and leave the walls thick enough that they do not need support.

After each step is removed, it will help if you rough sand the area down to 240 grit before moving on, especially if the wood is being turned green. If you leave it until you have finished turning, the bowl may have warped. As with the outside of the bowl, take care not to soften the crispness of the edge. This is slightly more difficult on the inside as the surface is concave and access is restricted.

Hold the abrasive so that the cloth forms a curve. Your left hand should cup your right, covering any fingers that are not being used to grip the cloth, and

Fig 12.12 *During the final finishing cuts, the outside of the bowl may need supporting to prevent the wood flexing away from the tool. Take care not to catch your hand on the spinning edges.*

Woodturning Courses
with
Robert Chapman

Learn from a professional woodturner with twelve years experience

1, 2, 3 & 5 day courses or regular evening sessions over a number of weeks

Maximum of two students per course

Full hands on tuition in a clean and fully equipped workshop

Courses tailored to suit all levels from complete beginners to advanced and beyond

Enrol now and learn to turn with the author of "Woodturning: A Fresh Approach"

For full details of courses please return tear off slip

Robert Chapman 93 Park Way, Coxheath, Maidstone, Kent, ME17 4EX.
Telephone/fax 01622 747325

✂ — — — — — — — — — —

Please send me details of woodturning courses

Name ....

Address ....

....

....

Post code .... Tel ....

Fig 12.13 *When sanding the inside, your left hand should cup your right, and you should keep both elbows against your body. This will provide a very stable grip, which will help resist any downward force against the cloth.*

both elbows should be kept tight into your body. This will provide a very stable grip, enabling you to resist any downward force against the cloth (see Fig 12.13).

By holding the abrasive gently against the spinning wood at a depth of 1in (25mm) or more and then drawing it slowly out of the bowl and past the edge, the chances of rounding over the leading edges of the rim are reduced. Remember to keep the cloth moving in order to avoid creating any ridges, and keep account of where your hand is in relation to the sharp spinning edge.

Continue turning deeper into the bowl in the same way, working in small steps and checking the

thickness each time before moving on. As you get deeper into the bowl, you will often be forced to use callipers to gauge the thickness as your fingers will no longer reach. If you are willing to take the wall thickness fairly thin, you may also be able to use the light that filters through the edge as a guide to wall thickness (see Fig 12.14).

As you get further over the rest, you will find that the ¼in (6mm) gouge is no longer effective as it will vibrate. At this point you are normally forced to change to the ⅜in (10mm) and sometimes the ½in (13mm) gouge, continuing as before, taking the finest cuts that you can when finishing. When you reach the

Fig 12.14 *If the bowl is thin enough, the wall thickness can sometimes be accurately judged by the amount of light coming through the sides.*

Fig 12.15 *When the bevel on a conventional tool begins to lose contact with the wood, an angled bowl gouge can be used to finish the bottom.*

bottom of the bowl, you will often find that the tool starts to jump around. This is because the bevel is no longer able to make contact with the wood, as the sides of the bowl prevent the handle from being correctly positioned. If you try to cut the wood in this way, you will not be able to control the tool effectively, and the surface finish will suffer. At this stage I prefer to use an angled bowl gouge by BCWA. This has the end of the tool bent round at 30° to the shaft to enable the bevel to stay in contact with the work in awkward areas (see Fig 12.15). When this is used with the flute on its side, fine finishing cuts are possible at the bottom of deep-sided bowls.

Alternatively, you could keep one gouge ground with a very flat bevel of about 5° just for the base of deeper bowls. This will enable the bevel to remain in contact with the work, though with such a short bevel, the finish may need more attention afterwards.

If the bottom has been cut with a straight bowl gouge, any remaining ridges can be removed with a light pass from a ½in (13mm) round-nose scraper. Set the tool rest so that the tip of the scraper is cutting above centre line: this will ensure that any force from the wood pushes the tool away from the work. If the rest is set too low and the scraper is cutting below centre line, the force of the wood on the tool will tend to drag the cutting edge deeper into the work with disastrous consequences. You should also aim to

keep the tool over on its side, about 45° anti-clockwise. This cushions the force of the cutting edge against the wood, producing a shear scraping effect as described in Chapters 4 and 6 (see Figs 4.16 and 6.9, pages 42 and 60). If the tool is held flat on the rest, the downward force on the surface is much greater and you risk tearing the fibres of the wood.

The bottom of the bowl can now be sanded, and any final sanding of the upper areas can also be done. Sanding the bottom of the inside can be quite tricky if the bowl is fairly deep or narrow.

The natural edge also creates its own problems, as the spinning edge can be quite sharp. If your hand comes into contact with it you will very quickly be made aware of the fact by a sudden pain that you will remember for some time. To solve this problem, I use velcro-backed power sanding discs attached to the end of a length of dowel (see Fig 1.17, page 11). I support the dowel with the tool rest while I safely sand the inside smooth (see Fig 12.16).

Turning the foot

The base of the outside can now be blended into the previously turned surface, using a ¼in (6mm) bowl gouge. Turn the foot of the bowl to create a concave radius in the base (see Fig 12.17).

Remember that you are working cross-grained timber, so try to work with the flute facing towards you and cutting away from the headstock. If this proves difficult because of the restricted access, use a ⅜in (10mm) spindle gouge with swept back sides and take the finest of cuts working the other way, cutting against the grain.

If necessary you can then draw the gouge towards you, keeping it on its side in a scraping action, to further refine the surface. Any details in the foot, such as the small shoulder on this piece where the foot

meets the upper profile, should also be turned using the spindle gouge (see Fig 12.18).

Now, finish sand and polish the foot along with the inside. One cautionary note; if you are using wire wool around the natural edges, stop the lathe and rub the surface while the work is stationary. If you don't stop the lathe, you risk damaging the edges of the bowl *and* your fingers. As an alternative, you can cut back the surface with 1200 grit silicone carbide paper.

Fig 12.16 *A velcro-backed sanding disc attached to a length of dowel is a useful aid when sanding in awkward areas.*

Fig 12.17 *The foot of the bowl is created with light cuts from a ¼in (6mm) bowl gouge.*

For the same reasons as above, when you are polishing the bowl with a cloth, turn the lathe off and polish while the piece is stationary when you are working near the rim.

If the bowl is to be reverse turned to hollow out the foot, follow one of the methods in Chapter 19 (see Figs 19.12–19.15, pages 201–203). If not, all that is left is to part off the bowl from the waste wood. I advise you to select a low speed for this operation, in case the bowl is forced off when you do not expect it.

Using a ³⁄₃₂in (2mm) fluted parting tool, so as not to tear the fibres too much, cut through the base, stopping short of the centre by at least ¹⁄₂in (13mm). Saw through the remainder, with the work stationary, using a fine-toothed hacksaw blade.

Gently pare away the small spigot left in the centre using the tip of a ¹⁄₂in (13mm) curved carving gouge (the end of a sharp skew chisel or spindle gouge will do), before sanding the foot smooth using a 2in (51mm) sanding disc mounted in the lathe.

Fig 12.18 *Small, intricate details should be turned with the ³⁄₈in (10mm) spindle gouge.*

Fig 12.19 *The finished bowl shown relative to its original position in the log.*

GALLERY

In this second collection, the bowls are not always so closely related to the projects in the previous chapters as they were in the first Gallery. I have arranged the examples in an order that relates loosely to the designs used in the projects. However, there will be a degree of repetition in the techniques used to make the bowls. It is when these basic techniques are combined with the complexity of the infinite number of designs that are possible, that you begin to realize the scale of opportunity that awaits you.

The addition of a small foot is just enough to raise the bowl slightly from the surface, creating a more pronounced effect.

Spalted beech. Diameter: 8in (203mm).
The spalting occurred naturally on this piece, giving a very even effect.

Australian tiger myrtle. Diameter: 8in (203mm).
These striped markings convey a sense of jungle and safari.

Claro walnut. Diameter: 10in (254mm).
The figure on the face of this bowl is almost storm-like.

*Elegant details turned into
the foot will improve
the status of a design.*

Oak. Diameter: 12in (305mm).
*This nesting bowl was turned from the crotch of the tree while still partly wet and allowed to move.
The centre has been lightly coloured to enhance the feathered figure.*

Bird's eye maple. Diameter: 8in (203mm).
For maximum effect, the edges of the nesting bowl should be kept as crisp as possible.

*The naturally coloured rim
of this bird's eye maple
bowl provides a
contrasting frame to the
brightly stained centre.*

Beech burr. Diameter: 8in (203mm).
It is unusual to find a burr on a beech tree. This example also displays additional water staining.

Spalted sycamore. Diameter: 10in (254mm).
The black zone lines across the face of this bowl are made more interesting by their double-edged effect and irregularity.

This close-up of the underside shows the wonder of the natural spalting lines clearly. Notice the crisp line of the recessed foot.

Bog oak. Diameter: 7½in (190mm).
The medullary rays provide a wonderful display as they spiral around this quarter sawn bowl.

Turned complete when wet, bog oak is a difficult wood to sand. But then it has been buried for around 5,000 years.

Quilted American rock maple with coloured centre. Diameter: 10in (254mm).
The addition of colour gives a stormy effect to this pale but highly figured timber.

Yellow box burr. Overall diameter: 11in (280mm).
The nesting bowl technique has been combined with a natural-edged rim to give a variation to the theme. The contrasting colours between heartwood and sapwood are made more interesting by the burred figure.

Jarrah burr. Overall diameter: 18in (457mm).
Notice how the inner rim has been positioned to make the best use of the change in colour between heart and sapwood.

Sycamore. Diameter: 9in (229mm).
The patchy markings of this sycamore bowl are a result of drying the timber flat instead of on end, as sycamore should ideally be end reared (see Chapter 2, page 26).

Subtle decoration in the base provides interest underneath.

Bog oak (wet turned). Diameter: 7in (178mm).
Turned complete while still wet, and dried afterwards.

Elm burr. Diameter: 7in (178mm).
The burr figure has opened up during seasoning to produce a star-like effect.

View showing silhouette.

Spalted beech. Diameter: 13in (330mm).
*Just because you can make a thin-walled bowl does not mean you should.
Sometimes a more chunky design is called for.*

*Close-up of markings and
rim detail. (The spalting
was artificially cultured
after rough turning.)*

**Masur birch.
Diameter: 6in (152mm).**
*Using the full half log of
this masur birch gives the
appearance of hundreds
of silvery streaks rushing
towards the centre.*

**Australian tiger myrtle.
Diameter: 5½in (140mm).**
A slightly closed form raised on a small foot helps show off this highly figured timber.

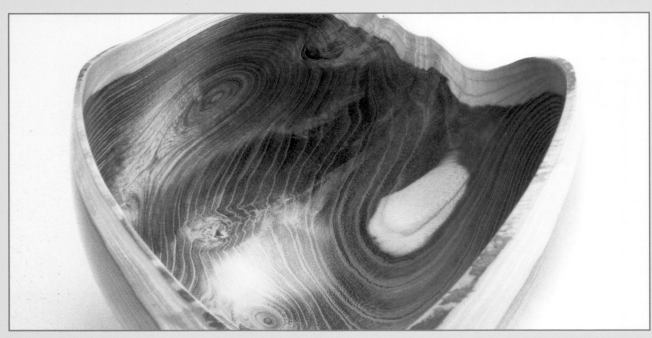

Laburnum. Diameter: 6in (152mm).
By using the crotch of the tree you will end up with three hearts in the bowl, along with some wild patterns.

Using the full diameter of the trunk enables the sapwood to follow around the outside of the profile and into the foot.

Cherry burr. Diameter: 5½in (140mm).
Notice how the small bark inclusions give more interest to the burred area than just the wavy figure alone.

Acacia burr. Diameter: 5½in (140mm).
The black line between the heartwood and sapwood provides an immediate focal point.

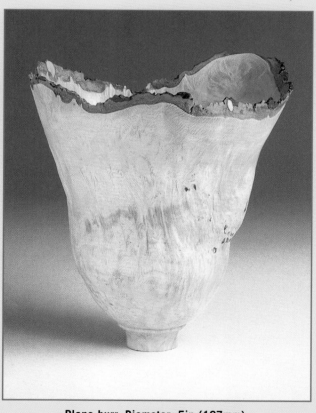

Plane burr. Diameter: 5in (127mm).
Working with fresh felled timber can be very rewarding as nature gets to have a large say in what the final shape will be.

From left: Elm burr, blackboy (grass root) and field maple burr. Largest diameter: 8in (203mm).
The dark rims on these flared designs are a valuable asset.

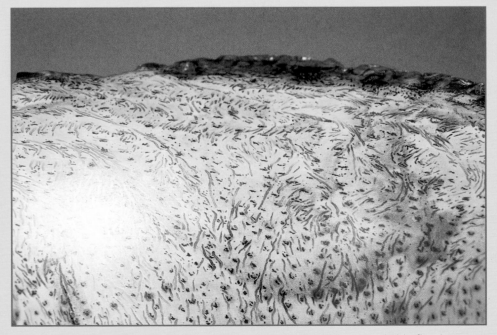

While blackboy is not strictly a wood, it does display some remarkable figuring.

PART FOUR

Hollow Vessels

in preparation

IT IS HOLLOW TURNING THAT PROVIDES the biggest attraction for me. The shapes are always graceful, and their only function is to hold your attention and enhance your surroundings. This means that more freedom in design is possible.

Since the mid-1970s, when David Ellsworth first drew attention to hollow turning, very little has been written about the subject. There will be many among you who ask the question, 'Why should I bother with hollowing techniques when I can't even see inside to judge the result? And anyhow I am quite happy making different shaped bowls.' This question has many answers. For most woodturners, even those who are experienced at hollow turning, there is nothing more challenging – each piece is its own reward. You get a feeling of excitement, an almost magical experience, when you hold a successful, thin-walled hollow form that has a hole you can hardly see into.

Every woodturner should learn at least the basics of hollow turning even if they do only wish to make bowls. After all, if you can create thin walls when you can't even see the tool cutting, imagine how easy it will be to turn a thin-walled bowl afterwards.

Design

When creating hollow vessels, simplicity is the key, with graceful, flowing lines that are easy on the eye leaving an uncluttered surface. For your first attempts, the vessel should be taller than it is wide, with a fairly gentle curve up the sides – rather like a flat-ended rugby ball (see Fig 13.1). This will allow the inside to be removed reasonably easily without the need for excess undercutting around the rim. The opening should be quite large to begin with, to allow the shavings to be removed quickly and to allow greater tool manoeuvrability inside. After you have gained a little experience, the profile can be flattened out to give a more squashed shape (see Fig 13.2). This profile requires a lot more undercutting of the rim, but it is a useful shape if the work is to be displayed low down.

Fig 13.1 *For practising hollowing techniques, a tall shape with steep sloping sides around the opening, similar to this sycamore vessel, will be easiest.*

Fig 13.2 *A shallow profile, such as this North American maple burr vessel, is far more demanding than a tall, steep shape and will require a lot of undercutting.*

Specialist tooling

For roughing out the bulk of the waste a straight tool is suitable. If necessary, existing tools can be modified to make these. A bowl gouge can be ground on the left-hand side to give a longer bevel (see Fig 13.3; see also Fig 1.13, page 8) and used to rough out some of the waste wood. The tool can then be used on its side (with the flute facing to the left) and the wood cut away in a scraping fashion. However, I find roughing out with this method a bit fierce. A ⅜in (10mm) hollowing Mole provides a more efficient and less intimidating alternative. While this is available commercially, you could make your own by regrinding the end of a square-section beading and parting tool. However, you won't be able to use the Mole (commercial or home-made) as far over the tool rest as the bowl gouge, because of its smaller section.

After the central area has been removed, the vessel must be undercut, and for this, specialist tooling is essential. Most of the popular designs consist of a

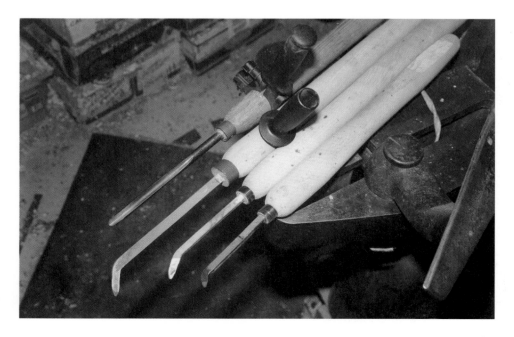

Fig 13.3 *My first basic hollowing kit consisted of a modified bowl gouge for roughing out and some forged angled tools for working in the side of hollow vessels.*

straight shaft with a cutting tip positioned at 45°. When I first started hollowing there were no tools available commercially, so I had to make my own. My first hollowing tools were quite basic, but adequate at the time. They consisted of a bowl gouge with a long-ground bevel, and a series of forged angled tools. These were made from square tool-steel in varying sizes, with the ends bent to 45° (see Fig 13.3). As I progressed I had other tools made. These had removable cobalt/HSS inserts fitted into round-section bar. (Round-section tools are preferable to square-section tools as the edges of square-section bar tend to damage the opening of a vessel when the tools are brought into contact with wood during the hollowing process.)

Nowadays there is an infinite number of hollowing tools available from most manufacturers. Some have straight cutting ends for the initial roughing process and some have cutting edges fixed at an angle for use in undercutting and finishing, while others have movable ends, allowing the tip to be used in either a straight or an angled position. Some movable-tip tools also allow the amount of side overhang to be adjusted to suit different shaped vessels and so keep radial torque to a minimum.

Choice of tool is a matter of personal preference. For the methods and projects described, I will concentrate only on those tools which have small cutting tips – ¼in (6mm) or less – set at an angle to the main shaft. Tools that use a large tip may be popular with some woodturners, but I prefer smaller tips, as the force produced at the end of the handle is directly proportional to the size of cut in the wood.

I have shown a few of the hollowing tools available from BCWA in Chapter 1 (see Fig 1.16, page 10). Other suitable angled tools are those designed by David Ellsworth, Melvyn Firmager and Chris Stott to list but a few (see Fig 13.4; see also Fig 18.4, page 178).

At this stage it is worth mentioning basic measuring equipment. With most hollow vessels, unless you have a large number of holes from bark inclusions, you will not be able to judge thickness accurately until you have had quite a lot of experience, and even then it helps to double-check. Callipers are essential but need not be expensive; even a piece of stout wire bent to shape will act as a rough guide. A depth gauge is also necessary to ensure that you don't cut too deep as you near the base of the piece (see Fig 13.5).

Clearing shavings out regularly is a common task as you hollow out the centres. Often shavings stick to the side and these need to be scraped out. For this I use a spoon taped to the end of a length of dowel (see Fig 13.5). When this will not fit through the opening, I use a length of wire to loosen the shavings. Compressed air is very useful, providing a quick means of blowing the shavings out through small holes. It is especially useful after the final hollowing cuts have been taken, when it can be used to blast out any dust and debris remaining inside, but be sure to use eye protection when using compressed air.

Handles

When hollowing out a vessel, the tip of the tool will overhang the tool rest much further than you would normally encounter in other areas of woodturning. As a result, the upward force on the handle is greatly increased, and this effect is intensified as the size of the cutting tip increases. To overcome this extra force, longer handles are needed, though how long will

Fig 13.4 *Various angled tools are available for hollowing, including (from left): BCWA twin position tool; contemporary editions of the original tools designed by David Ellsworth in 1975; and Melvyn Firmager's right-angle tool with top guide.*

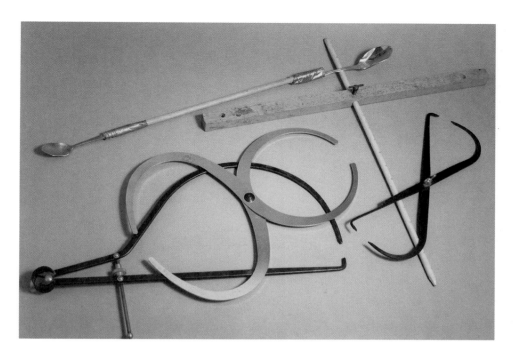

Fig 13.5 *A depth gauge and callipers will be needed to check the wall thickness. Note how the left-hand edge of the bow tie callipers is ground away to allow it to enter small-holed vessels.*

depend upon your personal preference. As a rough guide, I fit ½ and ⅝in (13 and 16mm) tools (having ¼in (6mm) inserts) with handles about 24in (610mm) long. I then fit these with a top handle about 5in (127mm) back from the ferrule (see Fig 13.3). These top handles are usually old side handles from power drills: they have a clamping diameter the same as most of my tool handles. Some tools I fit with a top handle of dowel – 5in (127mm) long and 1in (25mm) in diameter – secured with ⅜in (10mm) studding. It is not essential to have this extra top handle, but if a lot of hollowing is to be done it takes out much of the effort. With the handle on the top of the tool, you will not only have a more comfortable grip, you will also be able to resist any sideways torque on the tool. If the handle is on the side of the tool (to be used by your left hand) your tool control will be lost as your left hand will not be able to stay in contact with the tool rest to steady its position in the work.

Tool grip

How you hold hollowing tools will differ from what you are used to. Stand upright with your feet apart, as close to the axis of the lathe as possible. If you have a swivel-head lathe, it will help if it is rotated slightly. Hold the tool with the top handle (if you have one fitted) in your right hand and the long handle tucked under your forearm. The front of the tool should be guided by your left hand. For roughing cuts the tool may be steadied using an overhand grip but for

finishing it is essential that the front be guided gently by the fingers only, not the whole hand, or you won't have the sensitivity that is needed for the finishing cuts. Ensure that both the tool and part of your left hand remain in contact with the tool rest at all times. By keeping the handle underneath your arm, as shown in Fig 13.6, all the upward force generated will be absorbed through your elbow and into your shoulder.

For the roughing cuts it will help if a vertical pin, such as a threaded bolt, is fitted into the tool rest. The side of the tool can then be positioned against the pin and the pin used as a pivot point to enable the wood to be removed more easily (see Figs 13.7; see also Fig 14.2, page 148). This does not mean to say that you should use excessive force, merely that it will greatly reduce the amount of effort needed to hollow out the work. If you have not fitted a pin in the tool rest don't worry too much at this stage (I managed for about three years before I bothered to fit one), it just means that you will have to put in more effort to hold the tool during the roughing out process. The edge of the opening can also be used as a leverage point on harder woods, but only if you are using round-section tools. It is on natural, bark-edged openings that the pin is of most benefit as on these, the edge of the opening cannot be used to rest the tools against.

Safety

With all forms of woodturning facial protection is advisable, particularly with hollow turning and

Fig 13.6 *With an extra grip fitted to the top of a long handle, most of the radial torque can be resisted with ease. By keeping the handle tucked underneath your forearm, any upward force that is generated will be absorbed through your elbow, into your shoulder.*

especially while you are still gaining experience. If the wood has a small flaw in it that you have not spotted or you simply have a dig-in or go too thin, then a hollow vessel can easily explode in front of you. So before you wade on in with your hollowing tools remember, face protection is not a luxury.

While on the subject of safety, it is worth noting that during the hollowing process you will normally be standing at the tail end of the lathe. This means that you may be a long way from the stop switch. Should you have a disaster, the first thing you will want to do is stop the lathe quickly. With this in mind, I strongly recommend that you get an electrician to fit a secondary, movable stop switch to your lathe as mentioned in Chapter 1 (see Fig 1.2, page 3).

Basic cuts

Whenever you acquire new types of tools you should spend a little time trying them out to get the feel of how they cut. With hollowing tools this is best done where you can see the effect of what is happening, and not deep inside a dark vessel. Start by using each of the tools you have to remove the centre of a bowl.

The cutting tip should be slightly above the centre line of the work, and the tool rest should be positioned so that the tip is slightly lower than the centre of the handle. Now rotate the tool anti-clockwise a few degrees so that the tip is pointing down to the left slightly (see Fig 13.7). With the tool in this trailing position, any mishaps and dig-ins tend to influence the cutting edge out of the work instead of dragging it in further.

Cutting tips

If you are using tools with replaceable inserts, try changing the shape of the cutting tip and see what happens. A square-cornered tip with a sharp point (about 80°) is best for rapid wood removal during the roughing cuts, although the surface finish will be poor. If you grind an edge on all three sides of the tip, you will be able to cut in any direction when the tool is inside the vessel. A fully rounded tip is best for the final finishing cuts – it can even be rotated slightly in the tool for a fine shearing cut when working softer spalted woods.

For a general purpose tool, use a narrow-angle tip with a lightly rounded end. This gives a good balance between the two and is also better for those extra-hard exotic woods (see Fig 13.8).

Straight hollowing tools

Before starting your first practice cuts, make a hole in the centre of your bowl to the intended roughing depth. Position the tool rest across the face of the work and begin by using one of the straight hollowing tools. A tool with a shaft size of about ½in (13mm) is ideal to begin practising with, although later the tool size will be determined by the size of the vessel you are turning and the intended size of the opening. If you have a pin in the top of your rest, as described earlier, so much the better.

Enter the tip of the tool into the hole to a depth of about ⅛in (3mm). The size of cut can be increased with experience. Using an overhand (roughing) grip, swing the handle out to the right, keeping the tool in

WOODTURNING

YOUR INVITATION TO SUBSCRIBE

As a woodturner you are missing so much if you are not already subscribing to *Woodturning* magazine. Published every month, *Woodturning* introduces you to a friendly club where you can look over the experts' shoulders and learn from them. With articles by talented, expert authors to advise and inspire you, *Woodturning* is tailored to every level of skill and experience.

EVERY ISSUE BRINGS YOU

- Test reports to help select the right tools and equipment
- Technical articles to improve your skills
- The latest turning developments from around the world
- Projects to enjoy, whatever your level of skill and expertise

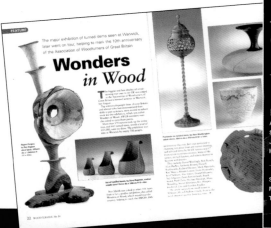

SPECIAL INTRODUCTORY OFFER

SAVE 20% on two-year subscriptions and 10% on one-year subscriptions

WOODTURNING

Fig 13.7 *The cutting tip should be slightly above the centre line of the work and rotated anticlockwise by a few degrees so that the tip is pointing down.*

a near horizontal, slightly trailing position, as described earlier, and watch as a small step of wood is removed. Continue in stages until you have removed an area about 3in (76mm) across to a depth of about 2in (51mm), then change to a tool with an angled tip.

Angled tools

Position this tool in the space you have just created, ensuring that the edge of the cutting tip is trailing slightly anticlockwise (see Fig 13.7). Bring the tip into contact with the work and swing the handle out to the right to take the cut as before, keeping the tool

Fig 13.8 *A fully rounded tip (left) is used for finishing, a square-cornered tip (centre) is best for rapid wood removal, and a narrow-angled tip with a lightly rounded end (right) is preferable for general purpose and hard exotic woods.*

against the pin. The cuts with the angled tool should be made so that each arc is cut to the same position and each one removes a step of about $\frac{1}{2}$–$\frac{3}{4}$in (13–19mm) wide from the initial diameter. Each new cut should take the tool progressively deeper into the work, about $\frac{1}{8}$in (3mm) at a time. Now change tools again, perhaps to a bowl gouge held on its side, and repeat the cuts to see how different tools behave.

After you have had some practice with the roughing cuts, remove the pin and use an angled tool to remove the wood. Your left hand should now guide the tool, using only your fingertips for sensitivity. The first finishing cuts are made in the same fashion as before, removing short arcing cuts. They should be made in forward steps of about $\frac{1}{16}$in (1.5mm) deep and swung in a short arc of about $\frac{3}{8}$in (10mm) (see Fig 13.9). It is these types of cuts that will be used to remove the remainder of the waste wood when working on a hollow vessel, to bring the vessel close to finished size.

Now use the angled tool to cut away the wood in a push-and-pull motion. Position the tool in the work and swing the handle to the right to pick up a small cut of no more than $\frac{1}{32}$in (1mm). Gently ease the tool forward by about $\frac{3}{4}$in (19mm), creating a small step, then introduce another small cut and slowly pull the tool back to where you began. This process is repeated to and fro as often as is necessary. These will be the finishing cuts used to smooth over the surface and remove the ribs left by the arcing cuts.

Spindle gouge

A spindle gouge used with the flute rotated slightly to the left can also be used to smooth over the ridges in

Fig 13.9 *Practise using the tools in a bowl to begin with so you can see what is going on. For sensitivity on finishing cuts, the front of the tool should be steadied with fingertip control only.*

accessible areas. This method is often useful on softer, problem timbers or just inside the opening where an extra fine finish may be called for. However, plenty of practice in an open bowl is needed before using the gouge in this way inside a finished vessel.

Straight finishing tools

Now change to a straight finishing tool and practise the previous arcing cuts, using the insert in the straight position. This type of cut will be necessary only when finishing the lower areas around the base of hollow vessels. To improve the finish in the base area on softer woods, it can often help if you rotate the tool a few degrees to give a slight shearing action. If you are working a long way over the tool rest this can also help reduce the amount of downward force on the tip of the tool. As you begin to work further away from the tool rest, you may find that the smaller-section tools start to vibrate. By slowing down the speed of the lathe, and ensuring that the tools are kept sharp, you will be able to push the limits of the tools slightly further.

When roughing out, most of the work will be done with a straight tool. However, when finishing the inside it is important to have the tip in its angled side position for as much of the work as possible. The very fact that the cutting edge has no radial support means that the cutting action is cushioned slightly. If a straight tool is used there is no cushioning effect, and when working on thin-walled vessels, the wood may be torn out, leaving either a hole in the wall, or, in

some instances, causing the work to explode completely. The only exceptions to this are when working on the base of a vessel or on shallow vessels, when access for an angled tool is restricted. In these instances straight tools should be used, as the back edge of an angled tool may catch on the opposite side of the interior wall as the work travels upwards past the tool. This would have disastrous results.

Practice

Once you have practised *all* these cuts with your different tools, try them all again with the tool rest positioned further away from the face of the bowl. This will simulate the effect of hollowing deeper work.

By practising in this way you will soon overcome any fears you may have had about using tools with an angled head. You will also discover which tools work best for you for pushing cuts, sideways arcing cuts, trailing cuts or pulling cuts etc. Using the tools to remove the centre of a bowl will quickly build your confidence. You will be able to see what happens at the cutting edge and how the tools behave before even beginning work on a hollow vessel. When you feel comfortable using the tools in a relaxed manner to remove the inside of a bowl you are then, and only then, ready to move on to the next stage.

In the following chapters I will describe various techniques that are needed to hollow out differently shaped vessels. These projects should not be rushed; take your time to practise and allow yourself to enjoy the learning curve.

practice vessel

I USE THE WORD 'PRACTICE' DELIBERATELY as no real attempt need be made to finish this piece successfully. It is merely a chance to try out what you have learnt so far, to use the tools inside a restricted space and to note any problems you experience before setting out to make your first finished piece.

Although much of what follows is similar to the design shown in Chapter 15, this piece should not be treated as a separate project, but purely as an exercise. It should be read alongside the following chapters and referred back to as often as necessary.

Roughing out

Rough turn a piece of straight-grained hardwood, about 7in (178mm) long, from 4in (102mm) stock, and prepare it to suit your chuck. The timber should be as cheap and uninteresting as possible, but free of cracks, so that you won't mind having to waste the finished practice piece. If you were to start by using a good piece of timber, with the intention of creating a finished item, you would find yourself under extra and unnecessary pressure. Until you have achieved at least a basic level of confidence, focus your mind only on the method of cutting and how thin the vessel is.

For all the hollow turning described in this book, I suggest you select a maximum speed of no more than 1000rpm to begin with. As you start to understand the different tools, so you may wish to increase the speed on some of the smaller pieces to suit your ability.

Refining the shape

After transferring the blank to the chuck, start by producing a simple profile, similar to that shown in Fig 14.2, then bore a hole in the end to about 4in (102mm) deep. As the object of this exercise is to make things as simple as possible to begin with, open out the centre hole to at least 1½in (38mm) in diameter, using either a rough hollowing tool or the edge of a spindle gouge held on its side. Working with a large hole will not only make it easier to manipulate the tools inside the vessel, it will also aid the removal of shavings. Removing shavings probably accounts for up to half the time spent on a vessel when working through very small openings.

After the centre hole has been widened the exercise can be made easier still, and more useful as a teaching aid, by adding a few large holes in the side of the work. Lock the spindle of the lathe and, using a spade drill, bore three holes, equally spaced down the side of the work and around the diameter (see Fig 14.1). These holes will allow you to see exactly where the tool is inside the vessel. They will also allow you to check the thickness of the wall quickly and accurately without the need for callipers.

Removing the inside

With the rest positioned across the opening, remove the first area of the inside. For stability I tend to use the largest tool that will fit through the opening, but for the initial roughing cuts of the first few inches inside the vessel I prefer to use a ⅜in (10mm) rough hollowing Mole. The small section of the tool allows more space inside the vessel for the shavings than if I were to use a tool with a ¾in (19mm) section. Using the Mole, or any straight tool with a square-ground insert, enter the hole and

Fig 14.1 *With the lathe spindle locked in position, a large hole is drilled in the side of the work. This will allow you to see where the tools are and what is happening inside the vessel.*

remove a triangular area about 1½in (38mm) deep. This should be done in stages, about ⅛in (3mm) at a time, using a sweeping action and an arcing cut as described in Chapter 13. During the removal of this first area, you will probably have to stop the lathe after every second cut to remove the build-up of shavings. Once you get further into the work you will find that the shavings simply fly out of the side holes made earlier (see Fig 14.2).

During your early practice pieces it will probably help if you follow the set sequence shown in the

Fig 14.3 *The inside is removed in stages, most of which can be done with a straight tool. Only area 7 needs to be removed with an angled tool.*

cutaway section in Fig 14.3 when removing the inside. By working in small triangular sections, each about 1½in (38mm) deep, you will soon be able to develop a rhythm, moving both your body and the tool from side to side to remove exactly the right amount of waste. As you progress deeper into the work, you may find that you need to use a tool with a larger section to withstand the amount of overhang from the tool rest (see Fig 14.4).

During the early roughing cuts you can normally estimate the position of the tool mentally quite accurately. This guesswork can be made easier if a few lines are marked on the top of the tool at 1in (25mm) intervals. These lines provide a guide as to the depth of the tool inside the work and this, coupled with the amount you have swung the handle around to the right, will give you a good idea of where you are.

Fig 14.2 *A roughing out tool is used to remove much of the waste in a series of arcing cuts. Notice how the pin in the far side of the tool rest acts as a pivot for the tool.*

Fig 14.4 *As you progress deeper into the work, and the amount of overhang from the tool rest to the cutting tip increases, you may find it necessary to use a tool with a larger section.*

The lines will also allow you to check that the tool is the right way up when inside the hole.

After the lower part of the inside has been rough turned to about $\frac{1}{2}$in (13mm) thick with the straight tool, the remaining area just inside the entry hole needs to be roughed out. For this, a $\frac{1}{2}$in (13mm) angled tool is used, with the insert clamped in the side position at 45°. The remaining waste can then be removed with a series of arcing cuts as described in Chapter 13. At this stage the work would normally be put aside to finish drying. For this practice piece, or if you were going to finish a piece green and allow it to dry afterwards, you should continue the hollowing process to finished size.

Finishing cuts

To finish the inside, angled tools with rounded cutting tips are used to begin with. Start by selecting a fairly small tool. I used a $\frac{3}{8}$in (10mm), twin position tool to start with but a $\frac{1}{2}$in (13mm) bar size would also suffice. On your first practice vessels, do not try to finish the wall thickness at less than $\frac{1}{4}$in (6mm). Enter the tip just inside the opening, pick up a small cut of about $\frac{1}{32}$in (1mm), and ease the tool forward around the inside for a distance of 1in (25mm). Continue cutting this area in a push-and-pull motion until the thickness is just above finished size, at about $\frac{5}{16}$in (8mm). The final finishing cuts should be made in the same way and taken for a distance of no more than $\frac{3}{4}$in (19mm) so that some of the previous step is left to be used as a guide for the next set of cuts.

After the initial area inside the opening is finished, you will probably find it easier to thin down the rest of the wall thickness by using a series of short arc cuts. Without yet putting on a cut, swing the handle round to the right until the tip touches the small area left from the previous section and make a mental note of your position. You should be about $\frac{5}{16}$in (8mm) thick at this point. Move the tool forward slowly until you feel the tip touch the step, then bring the handle back round in an arc to the left so that the cutting tip is just clear of the wood. Move the tool forward slightly to introduce a small cut and then swing the handle back to the right to cut out a small step, stopping at the same position as before. Repeat this action and continue cutting deeper into the vessel for a distance of about $\frac{3}{4}$in (19mm). Clear the shavings and check the wall thickness with callipers to confirm that it is what you had intended it

Fig 14.5 *The finishing cuts are made with an angled tool, using a series of short push-and-pull cuts along the inside wall.*

to be. Now take the wall thickness to its finished size and improve the surface finish using a couple of push-and-pull cuts (see Fig 14.5). Again, these should stop $\frac{1}{4}$in (6mm) short of the main step to act as a guide for the next set of cuts. This sequence of cutting in short steps and then finishing is repeated as often as necessary, working further round the inside.

It is important that you end each cut in a definite step and not just fade it out. As you get deeper into the vessel, these steps will provide a known reference point that you will be able to feel with the tip of the tool when picking up the cut after measuring the thickness with the callipers.

Continue hollowing in these short steps until you are within an inch or so of the base. At this point the tool should be used with the tip in the straight position to cut away the remainder of the wall thickness with short arcing movements, as described in Chapter 13 (see page 146).

When you get to the centre you will find that a small pip develops. This is because the effective surface speed of the wood at the centre is virtually zero. This pip must be removed carefully, using the straight tool at exactly centre height, coming in from the side. Use the waste wood in the centre of bowls to practise this technique. If it continues to cause problems, remove the remainder using a drill mounted in the tailstock at low speed. However, you should not let this become habitual as one day your vessels may have become too large for the drill to reach the base.

Depending on how you got on, you should now have a completed vessel in front of you. If you like the result you could always sand and polish the outside of

Fig 14.6 *After you have had a little practice, try the exercise again, reduce the wall thickness and maybe use a slightly smaller entry hole.*

the piece and save it as a reminder of your early hollowing lessons (see Fig 14.6). If not, try again and appreciate the fact that you have made the first step forward in the technique of hollow turning.

Developing your skills

During the early stages of your career in hollow turning, you will inevitably scrap a good many vessels – I still make enough mistakes of my own even now – but it is important not to become disheartened. Instead, learn from each mistake. If a vessel is not up to scratch, cut it in half (by hand, not on the

bandsaw) and study the inside to see if you can make any improvements next time. A lot can be learned by cutting a finished vessel in half, as shown in Fig 14.7. The ash vessel (on the left) was sacrificed out of pure curiosity. Although the section is not drastically uneven, it does thicken up quite quickly which adds unnecessary weight to the work.

With the field maple vessel (top right) the area just inside the opening is too thin in relation to the rest of the wall. The holly vessel (lower right) was taken too thin during the hollowing and had to be abandoned, although it does give an opportunity to show the steps left from the rough hollowing cuts.

Continue practising the techniques described in this chapter until you are quite comfortable with them. Each time try to increase the difficulty of the tasks you set yourself.

Move on to the projects in the next few chapters just as soon as you feel you are ready for the next stage. If you have any problems, just go back and refresh your techniques, using the middle of bowls to practise your skills.

The vessels that follow increase in difficulty slightly with each design. Take each task one step at a time and adjust the designs where necessary to suit your ability. As you work through them, you will find that each one will help you develop the various skills necessary to go on and create a whole range of hollow vessels. Once you have mastered the art of hollowing, the design possibilities are limited only by your imagination, and no longer by your level of experience.

Fig 14.7 *A lot can be learned by cutting a finished vessel in half.*

basic hollow VESSEL

15

Oak. Diameter: 5½in (140mm).
Height: 6½in (165mm).

A S THIS IS THE FIRST OF THE HOLLOW VESSEL projects, do not be too ambitious with the shape to start with. The curvature at the top should have just enough of a sweep away from the opening to provide a bit of a challenge when undercutting the top area, while the sides of the vessel should be made fairly upright in profile so as not to complicate the piece too much. A silhouette of a slightly stretched sphere is ideal.

For your early attempts, choose from a selection of straight-grained hardwoods that cut freely. Woods such as ash, sycamore and cherry are particularly suitable for practising. As you gain a little experience you can start experimenting with more figured woods to enhance your creations. For this exercise I used an 8in (203mm) blank cut from 6½in (165mm) square stock, with the grain running along its length. I chose a partially burred oak with a large knot and a few surface cracks in one side to give a little more character to the finished piece. However, I suggest you avoid wood containing any signs of cracks until you have a lot more experience and are aware of the pitfalls.

Roughing out

The first step is to rough out the blank between centres to produce a profile about ⅜in (10mm) larger than the finished form will be. Once this has been done, turn a dovetail in the lower end to suit your chuck (see Fig 15.1).

The profile at the base of the piece should be left about 2½in (63mm) in diameter at the moment, and often larger, as this will be needed to support the work during hollowing.

For larger work I will often just flatten the end of the blank and secure the piece directly to a 3½in (89mm) faceplate. This is my preferred method if the finished work is going to be over about 9in (229mm) in length, even if the diameter is only small, as longer lengths are better supported if attached to a faceplate, using at least eight suitably sized self-tapping screws.

Once the work is secured in the chuck, a depth hole needs to be made. This may be as small as ¼in (6mm) or as large as the intended size of the opening will allow. But remembering that the centre of the vessel is the hardest part to remove, due to its low surface speed, I tend to use the largest drill I can (see Fig 15.2). A larger hole capacity is also helpful to begin with, as it can accommodate more of the shavings produced by the hollowing.

For this first piece, I am aiming to end up with a vessel that has a finished hole size of no more than 1in (25mm) in diameter. However, while you are still finding your way with the different techniques, I would advise you to work with a hole of no less than 1½in (38mm). The depth hole should stop ½in (13mm) short of the intended finished depth. This small amount of wood will provide not only extra strength and stability when rough hollowing, it will also allow for small changes in the design later should the need arise. If you do not have a suitable drill, the hole can always be bored using a spindle gouge and then opened up with the side of the gouge or a straight roughing out tool.

Fig 15.1 *The blank is first prepared between centres to suit the chuck.*

Roughing out the inside

With the rest positioned across the opening, the first area can be hollowed out. To begin with, use one of the smaller, straight roughing out tools such as the ³⁄₈in (10mm) Mole. With the tool just inside the opening, swing the handle round to the right, taking about ¹⁄₈in (3mm) each cut and working from the centre of the hole out to the edge of the interior of the vessel. Continue working deeper into the vessel, as described in Chapter 14, until a triangular section about 1¹⁄₂in (38mm) deep has been removed (see Figs 14.2 and 14.3, page 148). Once you have cut away a small area you will find that the inside quickly fills up with shavings. These must be cleared regularly or they will become packed against the sides and grab hold of the tool, causing it to spin in your hands. The fastest way to clear the shavings to begin with, especially from small-holed vessels, is to blast them out with

compressed air (see Fig 15.3). Alternatively, you could simply remove the work from the lathe and shake the shavings out. If the shavings have become tightly packed, as often happens if you are working wet wood, they will need to be loosened first. This is best done by scraping around the inside with a long spoon.

Continue removing as much of the inside as possible, using the straight tools, to leave a wall thickness of about ³⁄₄in (19mm). While the thickness is not crucial at this stage, it is still advisable to have a quick look periodically to double-check that you are where you think you are. For larger vessels, or those with a high sap content, the thickness should be increased to allow for the extra movement during seasoning. Once you have hollowed the inside to a depth of about 4 or 5in (102 or 127mm), depending on the type of wood, you will find the smaller-section tools are not heavy enough to cope with the amount of overhang. At this point you should change to a tool with a larger section.

Once you have removed the waste from the lower part of the vessel you will need to change to an angled tool. Use this to remove the area of waste still attached around the opening. Enter the tool into the vessel, and using a series of arcing cuts, cut away the wood until the wall thickness is equal to the lower area. If the vessel has a fairly low, flat angle of descent around the opening, you may find it easier to remove the wood using a series of push-and-pull cuts instead.

As you enter the angled tool into the vessel, take care not to catch either the tip, or the back of the tool, against the opening. The same applies when you are withdrawing the tool. As you begin to gain more experience and start to reduce the hole size of the

Fig 15.2 *A chalk mark on the drill will act as a depth gauge when boring the centre.*

Fig 15.3 *Compressed air is extremely useful for clearing the shavings, but you must be sure to protect your eyes.*

vessels, it will be safer to switch off the lathe before removing the tool through such a restricted opening. This is another good reason for fitting a separate, movable stop switch.

Put the piece aside at this stage to finish seasoning. When rough turning hollow vessels, you will be able to take the walls much thinner than you would for a bowl of the same size. This is because of the ability of a closed form to resist the distortion and movement normally associated with drying wet or part-seasoned timber. As a result, your work will be ready for finishing much sooner.

You may wish to make the vessel in green timber, finish it wet and allow it to move. In this case, carry out the roughing process in exactly the same way, and then continue as follows without seasoning.

Finish turning

After the wood has seasoned, remount the work in the chuck and roughly true it up. Now study the outer profile closely for any imperfections that might force a change in the intended design before refining the shape to size (see Fig 15.4). The base of the vessel should be left oversize at this stage for support. When forming the top of the vessel, you should aim to create a slightly raised effect around the neck in order to leave a slightly concave area. This will give the opening of the work a more defined appearance than a single convex curve would.

With the outer profile completed, the rim around the opening of the vessel can be turned. Use a ¼in (6mm) spindle gouge to form a gentle, concave surface leading in towards the opening (see Fig 15.5).

Fig 15.4 *The surface is refined with a series of fine shearing cuts from a spindle gouge.*

Fig 15.5 *A ¼in (6mm) spindle gouge is used to form a concave surface at the opening.*

This sudden change in direction will provide a pleasing shadow on the rim when finished. Remember that as you are working on end grain, the last cuts should be made from the centre out towards the edge.

At this stage the outside must be sanded at least partially, to about 240 grit – more if working on wet woods. By partially sanding at this stage, if the work moves after hollowing it will still be possible to finish sanding by hand, with the lathe stopped.

Finishing the inside

When the outer profile has been rough sanded, the wall thickness inside the vessel can be turned to its finished size. Personally, for a vessel of this size, I like

Fig 15.6 *The inside is finish turned, starting with a ⅜in (10mm) angled hollowing tool.*

the thickness of the wall to be around ⅛in (3mm), though I suggest that you do not venture below ¼in (6mm) for your first half dozen or so vessels.

Begin the final hollowing at the opening, using an angled tool with a ⅜in (10mm) bar size, or similar tool. Insert the tool into the hole a short way and introduce a small cut (see Fig 15.6). Carry this cut around the inside for about 1in (25mm) using the push-and-pull method described in Chapter 14 (see Fig 14.5). Repeat the cut a few times until the wall thickness at the opening is about ⅛in (3mm) larger than the inner wall will end up being (see Fig 15.7). This will suggest to the viewer of the finished piece that the vessel weighs 'x' amount according to the *supposed* thickness of the work. However, with the wall thickness just inside the vessel reduced, the weight of the finished piece will be much lighter than that expected. Thus, you are able to create a pleasant surprise for the recipient. This illusion is particularly useful on larger work, when accurate sizing of the inside becomes difficult and you naturally tend to err on the side of caution, leaving more material in the bottom of the piece. The increase in thickness in the base of the work then evens out the actual weight to equal the supposed weight.

Repeat the push-and-pull cut several times until the wall, at a point about 1in (25mm) inside the opening, is approximately ¹⁄₁₆in (1.5mm) above the intended final thickness. I shall refer to these first cuts as the *sizing* cuts. At this point, take a couple more *finishing* push-and-pull cuts, though not quite so far, so that you are left with a step ¼in (6mm) short of the

Fig 15.7 *This sectional sketch of a typical hollow vessel shows the direction of both the sizing and finishing cuts. Note how the wall suddenly decreases in size as it drops away from the rim.*

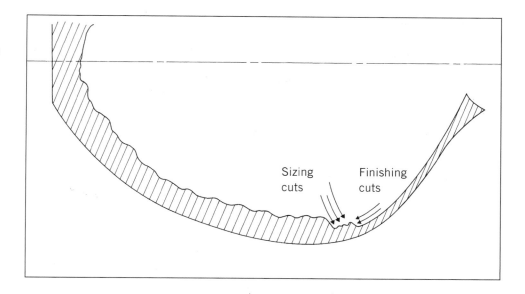

Sizing cuts   Finishing cuts

previous few sizing cuts. This should leave you with a double step inside the vessel (see Fig 15.7). After you have cleared the shavings and checked the thickness, pick up the sizing cut and continue a further ³⁄₄in (19mm) deeper into the vessel, still using the push-and-pull cuts to gradually reduce the thickness. Check the end point of these sizing cuts with callipers again before making the finishing cuts (see Fig 15.8). Take care that the finishing cuts stop ¹⁄₄in (6mm) short of this new step made by the sizing cut. If the finishing cut continues into the end of the step, you will suddenly increase the size of the cut dramatically and this would probably cause the tool to dig in.

When you have reached a point inside the vessel about 1¹⁄₂in (38mm) in from the opening, you will probably find it easier to change the method used for the sizing cut from a pushing motion to an arcing one,

as described in Chapter 13 (see Fig 13.9, page 146). You will also need to increase the size of the tool to one with a bar size of about ¹⁄₂in (13mm) or so as you begin working further over the tool rest. Continue removing the remaining waste from the inner walls using a series of sizing cuts made in an arcing motion, followed by the push-and-pull finishing cuts. Make sure that you leave a definite step at the end of each cut to allow you to pick up where you left off more easily.

As you progress around the inside, remember to keep clearing the shavings regularly and keep a check on the thickness with the callipers. While this constant checking is a little monotonous, it is necessary to ensure that you don't cut through the side of your vessel. As you gain a little more experience, you will find that you are able to build up

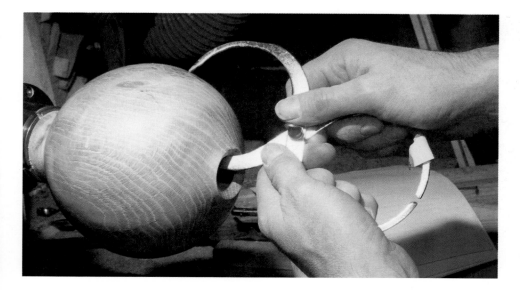

Fig 15.8 *Checking the thickness with callipers should help prevent you cutting through the side of the vessel.*

Fig 15.9 *Using a straight-edge at what will be the finished position of the base will help give a clear indication of how much still needs to be removed from the inside.*

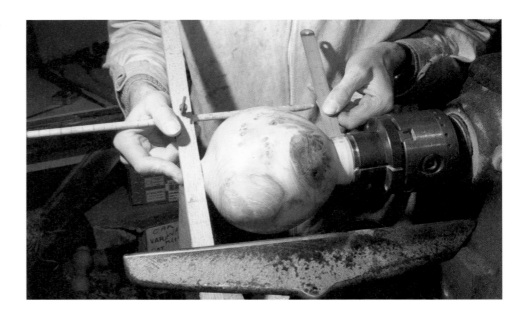

a mental picture of where the tool is. You will then be able to go around the inside much further before you need to check your position. While being able to judge the thickness in this way is very helpful, it is important not to become complacent and rely on it totally.

Once you begin cutting near the bottom of the work, be sure to change the insert of the tool to the straight position. The last part of the inside can now be removed with a series of arcing cuts, using a straight tool, and again finishing off with a push-and-pull cut over the surface.

At this stage you will need to check the thickness left in the bottom of the piece. This can be done quite accurately using a basic depth gauge to transfer the measurement to the outside of the work (see Fig 15.9).

When you have only the last inch (25mm) or so of the centre to remove, the cuts should be made from the left and the tip of the tool should be moved in towards the centre of the work, in order to remove the final pip as described in Chapter 14 (see page 149). I hope you have been practising this part on the inside of your bowls.

All the dust and debris from the inside must now be thoroughly cleaned out. After the shavings have been scraped clear and the surface dust removed, preferably with compressed air, apply the desired finish to the inside. Depending on the effect I am after, I will either use a matt black paint or a clear sanding sealer. I find the easiest way to get paint or sealer into the inside is to apply it using one of the spray-on aerosol varieties.

Fig 15.10 *The base of the vessel is blended in using fine shearing cuts from a ³⁄₈in (10mm) spindle gouge.*

Finish sanding and polishing

Once the hollowing has been completed, the extra wood at the base of the vessel is no longer needed for support. This can now be turned away and blended into the rest of the profile (see Fig 15.10). Next, finish sand the surface, taking care not to round over the edges of the rim as this would soften the finished appearance. Any cracks and fissures should also be sanded to remove any loose fibres and improve their appearance (see Fig 15.11).

After applying the desired sealer and polish, separate the work from the waste wood. This is best done using a fine-bladed, fluted parting tool with the lathe running at a fairly low speed. As the parting tool nears the centre, the work should be supported. If possible, this should be done with the tailstock, using

a soft cloth over the centre to protect the finished surface of the wood. Alternatively, you can use your left hand to lightly support the end. Later, when working larger or natural-edged work, it may not always be possible to provide support. On these larger pieces, stop the lathe well before you completely part off the work and saw through the remainder using a fine-toothed hacksaw blade. The small nib left in the base can then be removed using the end of a sharp gouge and the base can be sanded smooth with a velcro-backed sanding disc held in the lathe. Alternatively, the vessel may be reverse turned as described in Chapter 19.

Fig 15.11 *Any cracks in the wood should be sanded smooth to remove any loose fibres.*

Next steps

I hope you have managed to complete this first vessel successfully. Once you have had time to give yourself a pat on the back, why not try making a few more with slightly varying shapes, only this time narrow the goal posts a little by turning a smaller entry hole, thinner walls etc. If you are not that happy with the result you can always cut the vessel in half as I mentioned in Chapter 14 (see Fig 14.7, page 150), and use it to study the inside to see how you are progressing. This way, when you make your next hollow vessel you will know better how to avoid any mistakes. The experiences of this chapter should have given you a good grounding on hollowing techniques, enabling you to go on and try the shapes that follow.

Fig 15.12 *The finished vessel, ⅛in (3mm) thick – ¼in (6mm) at the rim.*

16

natural-edged hollow
VESSEL

Field maple burr. Diameter: 8in
(203mm). Height: 6¾in (171mm).

B Y NOW YOU WILL ALREADY HAVE PRACTISED
many of the techniques needed to create this
natural-edged hollow vessel. The outside
profile is turned in much the same way as the natural-
edged bowl in Chapter 12, and much of the hollowing
process is the same as in Chapters 14 and 15.
However, the addition of the natural edge and a lower
profile on the top face will just make things that little
more difficult. For instance, you will have to be
constantly aware of the position of the tools in
relation to the uneven edge, as well as where the
cutting tip is inside the vessel. With this in mind, I
suggest that before you start on this project, you make
sure you are familiar with all the techniques used to
turn the natural-edged bowl in Chapter 12, and with
the methods used in Chapters 13, 14 and 15.

You will notice that the grain will be running
across the work in this vessel instead of along the axis
as before. While this need not affect the way the
inside is rough hollowed, you may find that the tools
behave slightly differently when cutting the wood.
You will also notice that the two end grain patches
inside the vessel will have a rougher finish than the
rest of the surface. This gives you the opportunity to
practise cutting problem areas; you will need to use
sharp tools and very fine cuts to remove the torn

grain. Some woodturners prefer to use the tools in a
shear scraping manner when taking the final finishing
cuts, though I find that this is rarely necessary. The
shearing cut can be produced by presenting the
cutting edge to the surface of the work at an angle of
20°–30°. If you are using angled tools with movable
inserts, you can achieve this simply by rotating the
insert a few degrees in the direction of the cut before
taking the final finishing cuts. If you only have fixed
angled tools, it is possible to regrind the top rake
(top edge) to an angle of about 30°; this tool should
then be kept separate from the rest and used for
finishing cuts only. Do not forget to practise inside a
bowl first before attempting this type of cut inside a
finished vessel.

For your first experience with this project, I suggest
you start with a simple shape, similar to the one in
Chapter 15. After you have successfully completed
that, repeat the project using a lower, more squashed
profile similar to the design described here. By doing
so, and thus increasing the difficulty of the project,
you will provide yourself with a greater challenge; this
will improve your ability to hollow out efficiently in a
shorter space of time.

If, by now, you have developed a reasonable
understanding of form, then you may wish to consider
the introduction of more figured burr woods to
reinforce the effect of the designs. This is particularly
useful when turning natural-edged hollow forms, as
the irregularity of the surface will give a more
dramatic effect around the opening. For this project I
chose a piece of part-seasoned maple burr, 8½in
(216mm) in diameter and 7½in (190mm) tall.

Roughing out

After preparing a suitable blank, bore a hole in the
top so that the work can be mounted on 1¼in
(32mm) expanding pin jaws (see Fig 16.1). Rough the
diameter to a cylinder using a ½in (13mm) bowl
gouge (see Fig 16.2). Stop the lathe and study the

Fig 16.1 *Long pin jaws are necessary to mount the work, as the irregularity of the blank often means that the first inch (25mm) or so of the jaws is unable to enter the hole.*

timber for any features that may influence the design before continuing. Rough the base of the profile first, taking the cut from the base towards the headstock. When you have removed the bulk of the waste from the lower area, leaving enough of a foot to create a fixing later, start to turn away some of the natural-edged top. Depending on the type of chuck you are using, you will probably only be able to turn down to about a 4in (102mm) diameter at this stage. With the flute of the bowl gouge over to the right, make the cuts, working away from the headstock and cutting in the direction of the grain (see Fig 16.3). While this direction of cut is not essential during these early roughing cuts, it will give you the chance to practise working in confined areas and prepare you for some of the finishing cuts later. If you are working green wood and wish to retain the bark, then cutting in from the

Fig 16.2 *After the outside is roughed to a cylinder, the top and bottom corners are turned away at 45°.*

left will also mean that the bark is supported by the wood behind it. If you cut the other way, the bark may be torn away from the wood.

Once the profile has been roughed out, the foot can be finished, ready for rechucking. In this instance I used a glued block and faceplate. Using a 1in (25mm) square-ended scraper, with a shallow radius

Fig 16.3 *As the form develops, the surface should be regularly studied for any markings or defects that may affect the design of the vessel.*

Fig 16.4 *The base is scraped flat ready to take the glued block and faceplate.*

ground across the end to prevent the corners digging in, turn the base flat (see Fig 16.4). This must be checked with a straight-edge to ensure that it is either completely flat or slightly concave. A few shallow grooves cut into the base with the corner of a tool will help take up any excess adhesive when the wood block is glued on. Finally, turn the edge of the foot square, to a diameter of about 3¼in (83mm), to provide an alignment for the glue block. The blank can now be removed from the pin jaws.

Preparing the glue block

First, attach a block of sound, straight-grained hardwood, at least 1in (25mm) thick and 4in (102mm) across, to a faceplate. Roughly true up the diameter and face of the block before cutting a recess

¹⁄₁₆in (1.5mm) deep in the face. The recess should be opened up with a sharp-cornered tool until the diameter is just slightly larger than the diameter on the foot of the vessel (see Fig 16.5). This shoulder will allow the block to be accurately centred on the workpiece. Continue the cut a further ¹⁄₁₆in (1.5mm) deeper into the work so that it leaves a definite groove around the inner face. The face must now be scraped flat, in the same way that the foot was flattened off, and checked with a straightedge (see Fig 16.6). Again, cut a few grooves into the surface of the wood to take up any excess glue before removing the completed block and faceplate from the lathe.

The block must now be glued to the foot of the vessel using a suitably strong glue. For this I only ever use the cyanoacrylate glues (Hot Stuff) of medium

Fig 16.5 *A sharp-cornered tool is used to open out the recess in the wood block, to suit the foot on the work.*

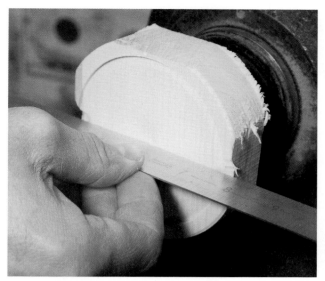

Fig 16.6 *Opposite sides of the block are gouged out to allow a straightedge to be used. If the face is in any way convex, the two halves will not fit securely.*

consistency. Apply the glue to the face of the block in an even spiral. Spray the foot of the work with an accelerator just before firmly pressing the two parts together. Using this method to hold the work is not only very secure, the curing time is normally less than a couple of minutes. I will often use glue blocks to hold work up to about 14in (356mm) in diameter. For peace of mind, all vessels over this size are always secured directly to the faceplate.

Remount the work in the lathe and reduce the profile of the work further, using finer cuts than before, until it is close to the intended finished size (see Fig 16.7). However, the base of the work must be

left large enough to support the hollowing process. If the work is to be put aside to dry out fully then the profile should be left at least $\frac{1}{4}$in (6mm) oversize at this stage. When refining the area around the opening of the vessel you may find the form more pleasing if you create a fairly pronounced neck – one that drops away from the top of the vessel parallel to the hole, then sweeps away in a curve to flatten out along the top face. This will help even out the ragged surface caused by the natural edge. If the profile around the neck were to flow straight out away from the hole you would notice a much more ragged effect at the opening. While this can be used to create a more dramatic effect at times, it should be avoided for the time being until you gain more experience.

Roughing out the inside

Removal of the inside always begins with the boring of a centre hole. For this natural-edged project there is already a $1\frac{1}{4}$in (32mm) hole, made earlier, which allowed the blank to be mounted on the pin jaws. However, you will need to make this deeper until it is within $\frac{1}{2}$in (13mm) of the intended finished depth.

After the hole has been drilled, the hollowing can begin. The tool rest should be placed across the opening of the vessel and (if fitted) the threaded pin should be used. Unlike in the previous project, the edge of the hole cannot be used as a pivot for the tool to rest against and so, for this vessel, the pin will be of great advantage.

Remove the waste from the first area inside the vessel using a small, $\frac{3}{8}$in (10mm) square-ended

Fig 16.7 *After the glue block is attached, the profile can be turned to its intended shape, leaving an allowance for seasoning if necessary.*

Fig 16.8 *The first part of the inside is removed using a rough hollowing Mole. Note the use of the pivot pin in the tool rest.*

roughing tool in a series of arcing cuts (see Fig 16.8). As soon as the first few inches have been removed and a space for the shavings has been created, I prefer to change to a ¾in (19mm) diameter tool. As the opening is quite large, this size tool can still be manipulated comfortably, and its extra mass provides greater rigidity during the roughing process. Next, cut away the lower areas in stages using a series of arcing cuts as described in Chapter 13 (see page 145). Remember to keep the shavings cleared and to check the wall thickness from time to time. Once the middle and lower areas have been removed, the waste from around the opening needs to be turned away using an angled tool of about ½in (13mm) diameter.

After the inside has been rough hollowed to about ¾in (19mm) thick, the piece can be put aside to finish seasoning. Alternatively, as I did with this example, continue working until the piece is finished, then dry the vessel afterwards and allow it to move. This approach is particularly useful on burred woods, as the surface becomes lightly rippled, giving a wonderful leathery effect.

Finish turning

Once the inside has been rough hollowed, the outer profile can be finish turned using a ¼in (6mm) bowl gouge (see Fig 16.9). These cuts should start at the opening of the vessel and continue around the profile

Fig 16.9 *Fine shearing cuts from the bowl gouge are used to finish turn the profile.*

as far as possible in a single sweeping motion. This will give a smoother flow to the line than a lot of short cuts would.

The underside of the profile must now be finished turned. Start near the base and come up around to the middle of the vessel. For these cuts, the flute should be over to the right and the tool handle placed as low as possible to give the greatest access in this restricted position. Using a gouge with a long side bevel will also help in these awkward areas. I hope you used the waste wood to practise with. Continue these cuts until the upper and lower profiles blend into a gentle curve.

Now sand the surface to at least 240 grit – more if the wood is wet. While power sanding is certainly useful on a vessel of this size, it is advisable not to use

it around the opening for fear of softening the crisp edges. Instead, sand the neck of the vessel with a piece of cloth-backed abrasive held firmly between your hands, as described in Chapter 12 (see Fig 12.11, page 121). When the outside has been partially sanded, you are ready to begin finishing the inside.

Finishing the inside

With natural-edged vessels, as I mentioned earlier, I often turn a more pronounced neck than I would for a vessel with a smooth, round opening. This means that the area immediately inside the vessel will not only be visible, but due to the size of the hole, it will also be accessible to inquisitive fingers. Therefore, the surface finish needs to be as clean as possible straight from

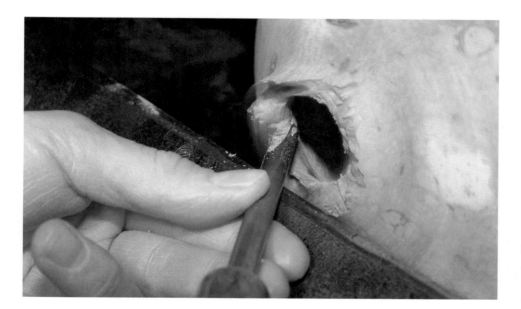

Fig 16.10 *By using the side of a spindle gouge with the bevel rubbing, a fine finish is possible.*

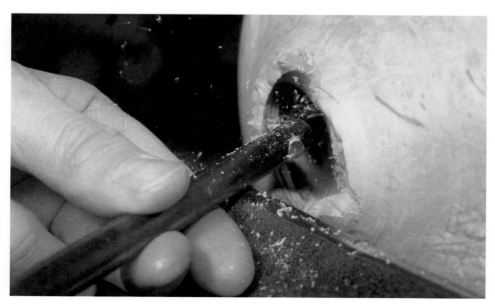

Fig 16.11 *A ½in (13mm) angled tool is used for most of the finishing cuts. Note the fingertip control for sensitivity.*

the tool. While it is possible to sand the area, as will be described later, sanding should not be relied upon to improve the surface finish when hollowing. As you begin to create larger vessels with smaller openings, sanding the inside will often not be an option.

To enable a smooth finish to be produced around the inside of the opening, I use a ⅜in (10mm) spindle gouge for the first few cuts. The gouge is ground with the left-hand bevel extended along the side of the tool for about ⅝in (16mm), similar to the side-ground bowl gouge shown in Chapters 1 and 13 (see Figs 1.13 and 13.3, pages 8 and 141). It is preferable to use the gouge so that the bevel is rubbing as shown (see Fig 16.10). However, until you are familiar with using the side of the gouge in this way in confined areas, I suggest that you rotate the gouge to the left an extra 30° and use it in a scraping fashion, which is much safer. The next step is to reduce the opening to the desired thickness, using a spindle gouge. In this case I worked to a thickness of about ³⁄16in (5mm). This is thick enough to prevent the piece from distorting too much as it dries, yet still light enough to convey a sense of fragility.

Once the opening of the vessel is finished, use an angled tool, in this case one with a ½in (13mm) bar, to continue the removal of wood (see Fig 16.11). Remember that the pivot pin should *not* be used for these final hollowing cuts. With the insert in the side position, pick up the cut where the spindle gouge left off. Continue this initial sizing cut around the inside wall for a distance of ¾in (19mm) before checking

with callipers. Repeat the sizing cut as necessary, as described in Chapter 15 (see Fig 15.7), then use the push-and-pull finishing cut to refine the surface before continuing further. Remove the remaining wood in the same way, working in a series of short steps around the interior as necessary. Once the halfway stage is reached, I prefer to increase the size of the tool to either a ⅝ or ¾in (16 or 19mm) bar for extra rigidity.

I know I have already mentioned this in the previous two chapters, but it cannot be stressed enough that it is easy to get carried away and forget both to clear the shavings regularly and to check the thickness of the wood – especially when you are working on free cutting woods such as maple. If the shavings are left, they will wrap around the tool causing loss of control.

As you progress further around the inside, you may find that your existing double-ended callipers are unable to reach due to the restrictive shape. If this does happen, you will either need to use pre-set, single-sided callipers or a piece of wire bent around to the same shape in order to accurately determine the thickness. As you approach the bottom of the vessel, remember to change to a straight tool to remove the last few cuts from the centre, then make a final check with a depth gauge.

If you wish to sand the interior you should do so at this stage, using a long sanding stick, as shown in Chapter 1 (see Fig 1.17). This is simply a length of dowel with a sanding pad on the end. It is used, resting on the tool rest, to reach deep into the vessel

Fig 16.12 *By holding the spindle gouge over on its side, a fine shearing cut can be obtained, to blend the base of the vessel into the upper profile.*

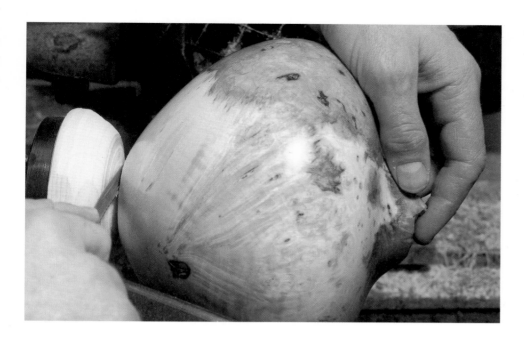

and can be safely inserted into the vessel, without fear of catching your fingers on the natural-edged opening. You could even make an angled version for vessels with a flatter shape.

After sanding the inside, remove all the dust and debris (protecting your eyes) and finish the inside surface with a spray-on finish. As your vessels increase in size, a spray finish may not reach the full depths of the interior. When this happens, the head of a brush glued, at an angle, to a length of dowel can be useful.

Finishing the outer profile

The lower part of the outer profile must now be blended in with that already turned. Due to the restrictive space around the faceplate, I prefer to use a ⅜in (10mm) spindle gouge to remove these final cuts. With the flute over to the right, the gouge is used on its side to remove light shearing cuts (see Fig 16.12). Begin the cut at the base and cut up and around the form, working away from the headstock. Using a gouge to cut towards you in this way takes a little time to get used to, so be sure to practise in the waste wood first. Once the lower profile is completed, the exterior can be finish sanded and polished.

The vessel must now be cut off from the waste. This is done by partially parting through with a fine-bladed, fluted parting tool. This is best done at a low speed to ensure that the work does not suddenly break away from the fixing. When the cut is within 1in (25mm) from the centre, stop the lathe and saw through the remainder (see Fig 16.13).

The remaining waste still attached to the underside of the vessel can now be removed, using a rotary burr held in the lathe. Finish off the base using a power sanding disc held in the lathe.

With this natural-edged vessel completed, you are now well on your way to becoming a competent hollow turner. Before moving on to the next project, go back and look at what you have done. Study the results and see how they could have been improved. If the hollowing is fine, is the form of the vessel as it should be? Does it bring out the best in the wood? Could you have used a better shape? These are questions you should ask yourself constantly in order that you may learn from every piece you make.

Fig 16.14 *The finished vessel, with a thickness of just under ³⁄₁₆in (5mm).*

vessels with spouts
AND LIDS

North American maple burr and Sri Lankan ebony.
Diameter: 8in (203mm).
Height: 4½in (114mm).
Spalted beech. Diameter: 5¾in (146mm).
Height: 6¼in (159mm).

U P TO NOW, much of what has been covered has dealt with both sequence and technique. The preceding chapters should have given you quite a good understanding of the techniques necessary to carry out most tasks, even if you do still need to practise them a little more. The following two pieces will allow you to do just that – practise. To add further interest they include a fitted top, one as a glued-in spout, the other as a separate lid.

With the spouted vessel I shall also be lowering the angle of the top face dramatically. If you follow the project using a profile similar to that illustrated, it should stretch your current abilities to hollow out a vessel to the limit. It will also give you the chance to use angled tools with long-reach cutting ends or inserts, even swan-neck tools if you prefer.

As many of the required techniques have now been covered, the following vessels concentrate more on the sequence than the method. This will allow you to use what you have learnt so far, and to judge for yourself the best method to cut a particular part.

By now the choice of wood suitable for your level of skill should be virtually unlimited. However, for the lidded vessel a close-grained timber would be a good choice as the flange of the lid will be cut across the end grain.

SPOUTED VESSEL

Rough turning

Mount the cross-grained blank, 8in (203mm) in diameter and 3½in (89mm) thick, on a screw chuck. Rough turn the base using a large bowl gouge, leaving enough of a flat to create a foot (see Fig 17.1). Once this is done, remove some of the waste from what will be the top of the vessel.

After roughing the profile, prepare a foot to fix onto a glue block and faceplate, as described in Chapter 16 (see Figs 16.4–16.6). Once the blank is on the glue block, refine the profile to within about ¼in (6mm) of the intended finished profile, then make a centre hole to within ½in (13mm) of what will be the finished depth (see Fig 17.2). For your first piece, this should be opened up to at least 2in (51mm) in diameter, as you will be hollowing out a long way under the rim.

Now rough hollow the inside in much the same way as described in Chapters 15 and 16. However, after undercutting the inside by about 2in (51mm) you will probably find that the standard angled tools no longer reach far enough, although this will depend on the size of the opening in relation to the diameter of the vessel. When this happens, you

Fig 17.1 *With the blank held securely on the screw chuck, a large bowl gouge is used to rough turn the base.*

Fig 17.2 *A hole is bored to within ½in (13mm) of the finished depth.*

Fig 17.3 *Various tools may be used when a long reach is required. From left: ½in (13mm) BCWA twin-position tool with long reach insert; long reach, square-section, angled tool; Robert Sorby swan-neck tool (modified to take a smaller cutting tip); and home-made, adjustable swan-neck tool.*

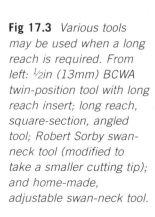

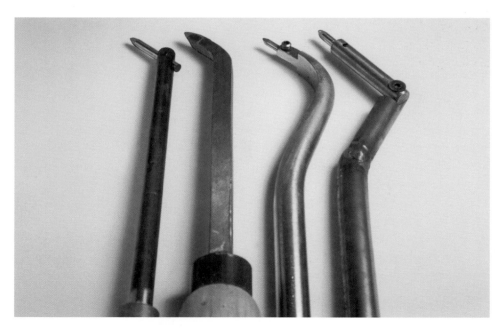

Fig 17.4 *When using swan-neck tools, the rest must be positioned under the straight part of the shank or the tool will twist. As with all hollowing tools, practice cuts should be done inside a bowl.*

will need to adjust the amount of overhang on the insert or even use an insert with a longer reach. Alternatively, you could use one of the swan-neck hollowing tools similar to those illustrated in Fig 17.3.

When using swan-neck tools, the rest should be positioned so that the bent section of the tool always overhangs it. This often means that the tool rest must be positioned about 2 or 3in (51 or 76mm) away from the face of the work. Used in this way, the tip of the tool will be almost in line with the shaft and as a result, the radial force on the tool will be kept to a minimum (see Fig 17.4).

When using them in confined spaces, take extra care not to allow the bent neck of the tool to come into contact with the right-hand side or lower section of the vessel. If the tool touches the opposite edge as it moves upwards, it will tend to lift off the tool rest and spin round inside the vessel. Unfortunately, the size of the swan neck on these tools prevents me from using them inside most of my vessels. However, occasionally I do find them quite useful on flat vessels with a narrow opening such as this.

After hollowing the inside to about ¾in (19mm) thick, put the work aside to dry. Unlike the previous two projects, finishing the vessel before it is dry, or part-seasoned at the very least, is not advisable. Once the spout is fitted, any movement in the wood will put tension on the glued joint and in some instances may cause the wood to crack or pull the joint apart.

Finish turning

Once the vessel is dry, remount it in the lathe and true up the outside. Next, turn the profile down to its final shape using a few light shearing cuts. Remember to leave the base diameter oversize at this stage to provide support during hollowing. Leave the edge of the opening slightly oversize as well, so that a final cut may be taken later after the spout has been glued in. This will ensure a smooth flow in the profile between the vessel and the spout.

A shoulder, which will be the fitting for the spout, must now be turned in the edge of the opening. This is best done with a square-cornered tool, such as a roughing Mole or a square-ended scraper. Open up the hole, to a depth of ⅛in (3mm), until it is about 1⁄16in (1.5mm) wider than the central hole. This will provide a small step for the spout to locate against (see Fig 17.5). To be sure of a good, clean joint when the spout is fitted, it is important to make sure that the sides of the shoulder are parallel. Partially sand the outside of the vessel before re-turning the inside to its final thickness.

As with the previous vessels, the inside needs to be finished in stages; first the sizing cuts, then the finishing cuts. Start from the opening, using an angled tool, and gradually work your way around the inside. Because of the flat profile of the vessel, it will probably be necessary at some point to use a tool with a longer reach to reduce the thickness (see Fig 17.6).

Fig 17.5 *A square shoulder is turned in the opening, to accept the spout later.*

Pay attention to the position of the tools inside the vessel, especially if you are using the swan-neck tools. It is easy to get carried away and allow the back of the neck opposite the cutting tip to catch on the lower part of the work while you are undercutting the edge of the vessel.

As you progress around the interior, do not forget to keep a constant check on the wall thickness. For a vessel such as this, I suggest you keep the walls at least ¼in (6mm) thick as you will need some support later when blending in the spout.

Once the vessel has been hollowed to thickness, clean out the debris and apply a finish to the inside. This is purely to seal the wood as the inside will not be visible once the spout is glued in position. Take care not to apply any finish to the shoulder as this will affect the quality of the glue joint.

Making the spout

For spouts I normally use ebony, but any contrasting timber is suitable. I never use the same timber as the vessel itself in order to create an invisible join.

Fig 17.6 *A long reach insert is used to allow the tool to reach the far depths of the interior.*

Fig 17.7 *The end of the spout should be turned parallel to suit the recess in the vessel. Note the small sizing step in the end of the blank.*

This would suggest that you are trying to pass off the finished work as something it is not – a vessel created in one piece, through a hole – and the recipient of the finished design may feel cheated.

I usually prepare a blank that is long enough to make two spouts as it is more efficient, saving time on preparing a blank the next time. With the blank secured in the chuck, face off the end square and turn a parallel diameter to suit the recess in the vessel (see Fig 17.7). The fit should be made so that the spout slides into the recess. If it is too tight you could end up splitting the vessel, too loose and the glue around the join will show.

Some of the waste from the top of the spout can now be roughed out. It is easier to do this now than after the spout has been glued in position. The inside of the spout should be hollowed out to about ¼in (6mm) thickness and the centre hole should be made

Fig 17.8 *Using a spindle gouge, the underside of the spout is hollowed out and the centre hole is bored to size.*

(see Fig 17.8). The hole is best made using the spindle gouge. The inside can then be removed using the back hollowing technique described in Chapter 3 (see Figs 3.7–3.9). Sand and polish the inside of the spout as part of this will be visible, then part off the spout and glue it into the vessel.

The spout must now be blended into the top face of the vessel. As most of the supporting strength has been removed from the work, it is important to bring up the tailstock to provide light support. The profile of the spout can now be turned to its finished shape (see Fig 17.9).

Blend in the base of the work, which was left oversize for support, before sanding and polishing. Cut off the work from the glue block and either sand the base or reverse turn it as described in Chapter 19.

Fig 17.9 *Using light cuts, the spout is blended into the top of the vessel.*

Fig 17.10 *The finished vessel in contrasting North American maple burr and Sri Lankan ebony.*

LIDDED VESSEL

Rough turning

For this ball-shaped vessel it is possible to do much of the rough hollowing using only straight hollowing tools. On such a simple form, you should concentrate on finishing the wall thickness more evenly, and to a thinner section, than your previous vessels.

When making a lidded vessel, I prefer to use the same timber for the lid and the vessel, in this case

spalted beech. If you make the lid from the base of the blank, it will allow you to use the wood efficiently and with a minimum of waste (see Fig 17.11). The plug of the lid can be fitted neatly between the screw holes where the blank is secured to the faceplate.

Start with a blank 6in (152mm) square and 8in (203mm) long, and reduce it to a cylinder between centres. Rough turn the profile and flatten off the base to take a faceplate. As the direction of the grain is running along the axis of the work, it is advisable to use extra screws to secure the blank to the faceplate: the fixing will not be as strong as it would be in cross-grained timber. With the work now attached to the faceplate, the profile can be turned to within ¼in (6mm) of its finished size. Rough hollow the inside and put the piece aside to dry.

Finish turning

Once the work is dry, the profile can be re-turned to its finished shape. Using a spindle gouge, turn a hard-edged shoulder between the main ball of the vessel and the base of the neck (see Fig 17.12). This should produce the effect of a collar at the top of the design. The neck of the work should begin to sweep out away from the ball of the vessel, immediately after the shoulder, producing a gentle, concave surface blending into a top with parallel sides. Rough sand the surface before going on to finish turn the inside.

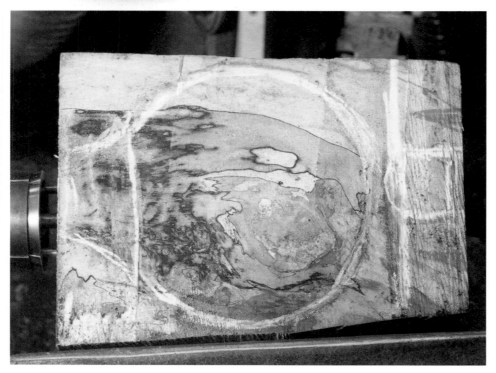

Fig 17.11 *The lid is made from the wood at the base of the work so that the screw holes are in the waste area around the plug of the lid.*

Fig 17.12 *The surface is refined using fine shearing cuts, leaving a step at the base of the collar.*

As the opening of the vessel is both visible and easily accessible, use a spindle gouge on its side to turn the first part of the inside surface. To begin undercutting the inside, select an angled tool and start the cut at least ⅝in (16mm) inside the vessel. This will leave a straight area on which to fit the plug of the lid later on. Continue hollowing the inside in stages, as described in the previous chapters, until the section is of the thickness required. The outside of the base can now be blended into the rest of the work before sanding and polishing.

After parting off the vessel it is a relatively straightforward process to reverse turn the work, as the inside of the neck has a large, parallel surface.

The neck can then be lightly gripped using expanding pin jaws. Alternatively, when the plug of the lid has been turned, it can be used as a jam chuck to drive the work, as described in Chapter 19.

Turning the lid

After the vessel has been cut off, turn a dovetail fitting into what will later become the top face of the lid (see Fig 17.13). Remove the faceplate and hold the lid in the chuck.

Next, turn the outer diameter to size and remove the bulk of the waste from the underside of the lid. Using a parting tool, turn in a narrow shoulder, ¹⁄₁₆in (2mm) wide, to fit into the neck of the vessel. Once

Fig 17.13 *A dovetail mounting is turned in the top of the lid before removing the faceplate.*

173

Fig 17.14 *The plug is turned to size to suit the hole in the vessel. Note the sizing step in the end of the plug.*

Fig 17.15 *When turning across end grain, fine cuts are necessary to avoid tearing out the fibres.*

you have created this short sizing step, turn the rest of the plug to the same size using the spindle gouge (see Fig 17.14). If you're going to use the plug of the lid as a jam chuck to reverse turn the base, this will need to be a push fit to begin with (see Chapter 19). The fit should then be eased so that it is just loose enough to allow for any movement in the vessel. Now turn the underside of the rim to size. Remember, you are turning across end grain, so be careful not to tear out the fibres (see Fig 17.15). Hollow out the inside of the plug using a small spindle gouge (see Fig 17.16).

While the lid is still being held in the chuck, the upper face of the rim can be partially turned. If the first ½in (13mm) of the rim is turned to thickness now, any small error in alignment when reverse turning will not matter so much. Following this, the underside of the lid can be sanded and polished.

Fig 17.16 *A ¼in (6mm) spindle gouge is used to hollow the inside of the plug.*

Fig 17.17 *The lid is held in wooden reversing jaws while turning the top face. Note the use of the flat-ended wooden insert in the tailstock; this is to prevent the lid slipping out of the jaws.*

To reverse the lid, my preferred method is to use a set of nylon self-turn jaws, or wooden jaws with a small recess turned in them to gently hold on the plug of the lid (see Fig 17.17). Alternatively, a jam chuck could be made by turning a hole in a block of wood to provide a push fit for the plug, as described in Chapter 19 (see Fig 19.9, page 200). With either method it is advisable to bring up the tailstock, just to safeguard against the work coming out of the fixing. Turn the face of the lid to size, leaving a small, raised step in the centre of the lid that is the same size as the outer diameter of the neck of the vessel. The flow of the line from the neck will then appear to continue into the lid, creating a balanced effect. The tailstock can now be withdrawn and the centre of the lid completed before sanding and polishing.

Next steps

With the two vessels completed, go back and repeat the two projects, but this time swap the designs. Turn a squashed, lidded vessel and a taller, spouted vessel and see how you get on. The tall, spouted vessel will not be that different, but with the lidded vessel, a tall neck on an already flat profile will make hollowing just that little bit more demanding.

Fig 17.18 *The finished vessel in spalted beech, with a thickness of ⅛in (3mm).*

miniature bark-rimmed
VESSEL

THIS FINAL PROJECT HAS BEEN INCLUDED to allow you to vary what you have learnt so far, not just so that you can create a vessel with a wide-rimmed neck, though this will prove useful when applied to larger vessels, but to give you a chance to venture further into a world of keyhole surgery. In the unlikely event that you ever become bored making the larger versions of hollow vessels, this exercise will soon put a challenge back into your work. Also, if you are intending to turn the vessel complete in one session, from fresh felled timber, you will need to work fairly quickly to avoid the work distorting before you have finished.

When working with such restrictions as encountered in this project – small holes and thin walls – you will be using all your skills to the full extent. It is inevitable that the scrap rate will be higher than before. For this reason, I suggest that you prepare a number of blanks to begin with and treat

each as a practice piece. If you use a variety of different woods, you will be able to compare the results. After a few attempts you will be successful, and you can then tell yourself, 'that was the piece I meant to finish'.

You do not have to begin by making a vessel with a bark edge. In fact, the first time you make a miniature vessel, I suggest that you concentrate purely on the technique of hollowing through a small hole. Then, once you have had a bit of practice, try to follow the project more closely.

Preparing the blank

To begin, cut a piece of wood about 4in (102mm) long from a log of about 2½in (63mm) diameter. If you use the bandsaw for this, remember to use a V block to prevent the round section from rolling into the blade. For this vessel I used freshly felled yew as it is easy to sand while still wet and will not move very much as it dries out. I often use eucalyptus or plane when green turning, and some-times burr woods, as the effect is more varied, but to begin with they should be avoided: they can be rather challenging as sometimes they move quite considerably.

The blank I used here was cut from the trunk. You can use branch wood to make the vessels, but the fibres in branches are under more tension than those found in the trunk. Such wood is often referred to as reaction wood (described in Chapter 2, see page 21). While the result can be quite effective, the work does have a tendency to warp to one side, quite heavily in some woods, and the finsihed vessel may be too one-sided to stand up.

Rough turning

With the blank prepared and held in the chuck, turn the profile of the work to size using a spindle gouge. For these smaller vessels, there is little to be gained by leaving the profile oversize at this stage. When cutting under the rim, it will help if you use a gouge with the

Fig 18.1 *The end of a hollowing tool can be used as a scraper to reach awkward areas. Note the extra wood left on the base for support.*

sides ground right back to allow you to work into the base of the narrow neck. As the neck is reduced further, access will become more difficult. At this stage, I prefer to use a hollowing tool with a round insert clamped in the straight position (see Fig 18.1). This can be used as a scraper to enable more wood to be removed safely. If the neck is particularly narrow, then the rounded end of a ¹⁄₁₆in (1.5mm) wide, Melvyn Firmager style scraping and parting tool can be useful (see Fig 18.2). With many species of timber, such as holly and eucalyptus, as the wood dries out, the greater shrinkage at the edge of the rim will cause it to rise up. If you had already turned the rim with an upward angle, you could end up with a disappointingly high neck line on the finished form. The rim of the

vessel should be left about ¹⁄₄in (6mm) thick at this stage, to provide support when turning the top face.

The top face of the rim can now be turned to size. This is best done in stages, finishing the first ¹⁄₂in (13mm) in from the edge down to thickness, then the next and so on. If you try to cut the whole face in one pass, often the wood will not be strong enough to support the cut at the edge. On more flexible woods, you may well find it necessary to support the back of the rim with your fingers. This will prevent it pushing away from the tool as the edge becomes thinner (see Fig 18.3). The surface must now be partially sanded before the hollowing begins.

Bore a hole to the required depth in the centre of the work, using a ¹⁄₄in (6mm) spindle gouge. For your

Fig 18.2 *In very narrow spaces, the rounded end of a thin parting tool can be used.*

Fig 18.3 *Use the fingers of your left hand to support the rim of the vessel for the final shearing cuts, especially when wet turning more flexible woods such as this holly.*

early attempts at small hole work, I suggest that you open up the hole slightly, using the side of a spindle gouge, to at least ³⁄₈in (10mm).

Rough hollowing

For small vessels there are very few hollowing tools available commercially that will fit through the holes. As a result, you may need to improvise if you wish to create vessels with holes smaller than ¼in (6mm) in diameter. A small spindle gouge can be used for some of the rough hollowing, and miniature angled tools can even be made from ⅛in (3mm) hexagonal socket wrenches, although not being HSS, they will lose their edge quite quickly (see Fig 18.4).

To begin the hollowing, use a straight tool to remove the first area in much the same way as for the larger vessels. In this instance I used a ¼in (6mm) spindle gouge for most of the work. Using the gouge with its flute rotated to the left about 15° from horizontal, enter the hole with the handle at an angle of 10° to the right (see Fig 18.5). Start the cut and push the tool down the side of the hole into the vessel. After a short distance remove the gouge, sliding it back out of the hole while keeping the flute upwards. The flute of the gouge will now be full of shavings; remove these before you repeat the cut. Continue the cuts as far as possible with the spindle gouge until access becomes too restricted. At this point change over to a straight, miniature hollowing tool. If the tool is used in an arcing cut it will be less aggressive on the wood than the spindle gouge, giving you more control as you get further over the tool rest.

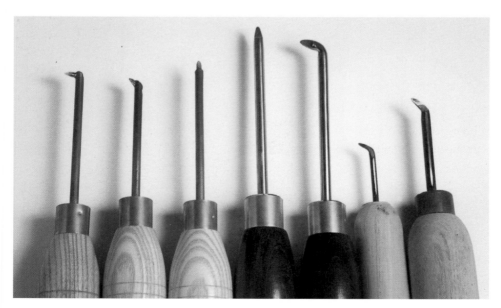

Fig 18.4 *Working through small holes requires small tools. From left: BCWA micro tools; Chris Stott miniature tools; and home-made angled tools.*

Fig 18.5 *A spindle gouge can be used to remove much of the waste from inside the vessel.*

Continue the rough hollowing cuts until you are left with a wall thickness of no more than ⁵⁄₁₆in (8mm). It is worth noting that when you are working with small vessels, the shavings will need to be cleared out and the thickness checked more regularly than with larger work. After the initial roughing is done, use a small-angled tool to undercut around the opening.

Finish turning

To finish turn the inside, start by using an angled hollowing tool. Insert the tool into the hole, bring the tip into contact with the wood, and slowly move the tool in and around the edge of the vessel (see Fig 18.6). The inside can then be finished in a similar way to the larger vessels, using sizing cuts followed by finishing cuts.

Gauging the thickness in the top area is not easy. During the early stages the thickness should be checked visually at the opening, and by using your mental perception to judge where the tool is relative to the inside. As you progress further into the piece, you will be able to insert the callipers to check the thickness more accurately. Repeat these sizing and finishing cuts until all the inside has been removed and the walls are an even thickness. Do not forget to change to a straight tool when you reach the bottom of the inside.

After hollowing is complete, the foot of the profile can be turned away and blended in. The outside should then be sanded and polished before parting off the finished vessel.

Fig 18.6 *A small, angled hollowing tool is used for the finishing cuts inside.*

This brings us to the end of the exercises. I do hope you have had a lot of fun experimenting with the different techniques described. And don't forget that if you turn through the side of a vessel, you can always cut the section in half to study the results. It is failures such as these that teach us the most.

Fig 18.7 *The finished vessel in yew, with a thickness of ¹⁄₁₆in (1.5mm) and a hole size of ⁵⁄₁₆in (8mm).*

GALLERY

This final Gallery brings together just some of the variations of hollow vessels that I create. Some are similar to the vessels in the previous five chapters, others quite different. You will notice that many of the designs have quite small bases in relation to the size of vessel. Because they are created to be admired, rather than used to keep anything in, I am able to concentrate entirely on the form of the piece, instead of having to worry whether or not the work is stable. As with the previous two Galleries, some dimensions have been given; these should be treated as approximate and are for guidance only.

**Spalted North American maple burr.
Diameter: 6in (152mm).**
Simple designs are often best when using highly figured wood.

Birch. Diameter: 5½in (140mm).
Bark pockets add interest to the pale surface of the timber.

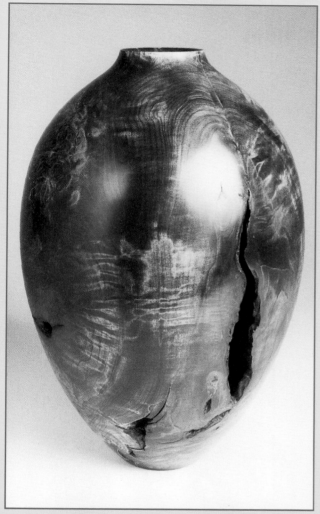

Coloured horse chestnut burr. Height: 12in (305mm).
The wood for this piece was cut from the crotch of the tree, providing a natural fissure in one side. The use of added colour changes not only the visual appeal, but also the mood of the piece.

Field maple. Height: 7in (178mm).
The surface of this straight-grained vessel has been radially textured, making it very tactile.

From left: Bocote, Osage orange, zebrano. Diameter: 3in (76mm).
Small-holed vessels may be challenging, but they are well suited to the bold exotic woods.

Coloured knotty ash. Diameter: 5½in (140mm).
By using the full diameter of the log, with the pith in the middle, the grain swirls around the outside of the vessel rather than straight up in vertical lines.

Gimlet. Diameter: 5in (127mm).
As well as adding interest, the natural holes allow you to see where the tool is when hollowing the inside. The down side is that the timber becomes more fragile to work.

Australian tiger myrtle. Diameter: 7in (178mm).
An inwardly sloping rim leads the eye gently down inside the vessel, and also gives the impression that the work is thicker than it really is.

Blackboy. Diameter: 7in (178mm).
Notice how the flow of the profile appears to be unbroken by the addition of a rim.

The outer diameter is probably darker because of natural staining due to mineral deposits in the surrounding soil.

Elm burr. Diameter: 8½in (216mm).
A black interior works well with the star-figured surface of this vessel.

Another view of the same vessel gives a completely different effect, showing a hard contrast between heartwood and sapwood.

Elm burr. Diameter: 9in (229mm).
This design combines many techniques, including those in Chapters 10, 12, and 16.

Coloured field maple burr. Diameter: 9in (229mm).
Look at how the ingrowing pockets of bark react against an otherwise near-perfect surface.

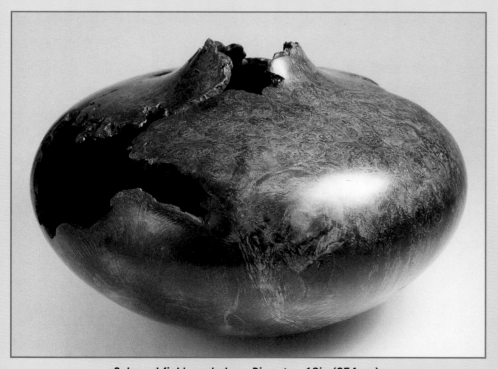

Coloured field maple burr. Diameter: 10in (254mm).
Some may feel that the natural beauty of this piece has been hidden by the use of colour. Personally, I like to view the surface as a canvas for further exploration, often generating a powerful emotional response.

Top view showing the balanced positioning of the natural holes.

Horse chestnut burr. Diameter: 22in (559mm).
The rim on this large vessel has been left quite thick – $\frac{9}{16}$in (14mm) – to allow the texture of the outer bark to contrast more with the smooth, turned surface.

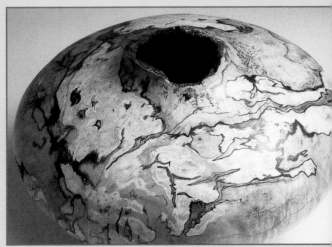

The spalting in the sapwood of this vessel was well advanced, making a clean finish difficult to obtain.

Rippled ash. Diameter: 11in (279mm).
The vertical ripple lines underneath provide a wonderful contrast to the spalted top surface, almost like rain from a cloud.

Spalted beech and African ebony. Diameter: 7in (178mm).
*Using ebony for the spout provides a relationship between it and
the natural spalting lines of the vessel.*

Yew and African ebony. Diameter: 4½in (114mm).
*The purple in this vessel was caused by the tannin in the wood reacting with the iron in
a barbed wire fence which had grown into it.*

**Coloured field maple burr and Sri Lankan ebony.
Height: 11in (279mm).**
A variation on the spouted vessel.

Beech. Height: 6½in (165mm).
*The point of focus on this vessel is the natural hole
in the side, which is made slightly mysterious
by the black interior.*

**Horse chestnut burr and
African ebony.
Diameter: 4in (102mm).**
*The creamy white finish of
the horse chestnut is
often dappled with small
pockets of bark.*

Oak burr. Diameter: 5in (127mm).
*Notice how the line of the neck carries through into the
top of the lid.*

Coloured horse chestnut. Height: 7in (178mm).
*The use of colour has transformed what would otherwise
have been a creamy white surface.*

**Spalted ash. Diameter:
5in (127mm).**
*This vessel, cut from the
crotch of the tree,
displays a wonderful array
of natural colour.*

Coloured horse chestnut burr. Height: 18in (457mm).
*The autumn colours applied to this lidded vessel help
convey a sense of movement, and the wind in the trees.*

*View showing underside of lid and neck
details. Notice the crisp edges throughout.*

Rippled ash. Diameter: 11in (279mm).
*While the ripple figure in this piece is quite pronounced,
the overall effect remains subtle.*

Wild cherry burr. Height: 14in (356mm).
This natural-edged vase was turned from the whole section of a log where a burr had formed almost right the way around the trunk.

Holly. Height: 5in (127mm).
The near pure white of holly allows the profile to be viewed with no distracting figure.

Papua New Guinean ebony. Diameter: 3in (76mm).
The dark lines provide a powerful, yet sombre effect.

North American maple burr. Height: 7in (178mm).
The delicate burr figuring works well on this thin-walled vase.

From left: Ash burr, buckeye burr, coloured horse chestnut burr. Tallest height: 9½in (241mm).
*By turning a small, flared base on the vase, the design becomes more stable
without greatly affecting the flow of the line.*

Holly. Diameter: 2in (51mm).
*The dark rim of this small, bark-edged vase provides a
powerful contrast to the otherwise stark white surface.*

Masur birch. Diameter: 4½in (114mm).
When masur birch is turned with the axis of the vase positioned vertically within the tree, a tear drop figure is produced.

Close-up of the underside showing the recessed base.

From left: Ash, laburnum, orange box. Diameter of largest piece: 2½in (64mm).
The same profile turned in different woods will produce different effects.

PART FIVE

Developing Your Work

reverse CHUCKING

WHEN I FIRST BEGAN WOODTURNING, the thought of reversing a piece of work just to remove the method of holding was almost unheard of. Even now I usually only reverse turn the work if it is necessary to the design of the piece or will dramatically improve its status. However, many woodturners today frown at the very thought of leaving any trace of the fixing behind, even if it has been incorporated as an elegant part of the design. Therefore, if you decide to turn the underside of your work, be sure to add a small detail that emphasizes the effort you have put in, such as turning a hard-edged recess in the base of a vessel or a raised bead on the underside of a pot lid (see Fig 19.1). More examples of reverse turned bases can be seen in the Galleries.

Whatever your reason for wanting to reverse a design and turn the underside, you first need to know the methods for holding the work. In this chapter I shall look at various ways of reverse turning, showing how some of the projects described earlier were reversed. Once you are familiar with the following techniques, you will be able to adapt the methods yourself to suit other designs.

Fig 19.1 *There is no doubt that turning the underside of a design adds status to the work. The two raised beads in the base of the lid definitely grab the attention.*

Fig 19.2 *Basic reverse turning can be achieved with little or no expense. Many applications require only a wooden friction chuck. Cup chucks can be improved further if made into simple collet chucks (top left).*

Fig 19.3 *If you do a lot of reversing then wooden reversing jaws are a worthwhile investment. From left: Stepped jaws for reversing flared and traditional bowls; ball chuck for reversing spherical items (note the step inside the rim for reversing pot lids); external stepped jaws for reversing bowls with a closed form.*

The most basic of reversing equipment, jam chucks or friction chucks, are made in the workshop. They take the form of wooden spigot chucks, to fit into the end of a hollow vessel, or cup chucks turned into the end of a block, to hold the plug of a lid (see Fig 19.2). For items reversed regularly, such as pot lids, a wooden collet can be made to allow for minor variations in the size of the work being held. For those who reverse turn a lot of different sized work, the Axminster four-jaw chuck, fitted with wooden reversing jaws, or with thick nylon self-turn jaws, is the most versatile (see Fig 19.3). Blocks of wood are screwed to the jaws and then turned to produce a series of steps, either male or female, depending on what is going to be held.

An alternative to the stepped jaws is to cut four quadrants of ¾in (19mm) plywood and in each, drill a series of holes radiating out in ½in (13mm) increments. Into these holes screw rubber bungs. These can be moved to suit bowls of varying sizes. If holes are made along each side of the plates, about 1in (25mm) in from the edge, you will have eight points of contact instead of four, giving a better grip on the work.

For more specialist applications, such as reverse turning spherical objects, a profile similar to that of the work can be turned into the wood jaws, providing a very positive method of holding the work.

Some items, such as natural-edged bowls and hollow vessels with bark edges, are difficult to grip

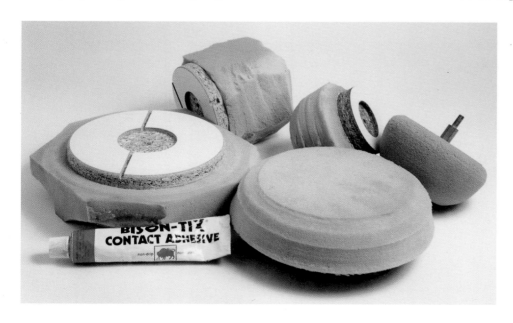

Fig 19.4 *Stiff foam blocks glued onto wooden backplates can be a useful aid when reversing oddly shaped work. Even the centre of an old drum sander can be used (shown far right).*

Fig 19.5 *A ³⁄₈in (10mm) parting tool is used to turn the shoulder of a jam chuck. Note the sizing step at the edge.*

in a chuck. For such awkwardly shaped pieces, blocks of stiff foam rubber can be useful (see Fig 19.4). The foam can be glued onto a block of wood, using contact adhesive, and then turned to shape. Soak the foam in water and place it in a sealed plastic bag. Freeze the foam overnight and the next day you will be able to turn in the required shape with ease. For large blocks that will not fit in the deep freeze, make them in the winter when the foam can be left out on a frosty night.

Reversing a lidded pot

Prepare a cylinder of wood, 3in (76mm) in diameter, to suit your chuck. If you make the jam chuck about 3in (76mm) long, you will be left with enough wood

to use again several times. Face off the end of the block and turn a narrow step in the corner using the end of a parting tool. Reduce the diameter of this small step until it is a push fit in the recess of the pot. The width of the step can now be increased to about ³⁄₈in (10mm) (see Fig 19.5). If you turned the step to the full width to begin with and then turned the diameter undersize, you would have to remove the full ³⁄₈in (10mm) step to correct it. On a small sizing step, however, any mistakes are easily rectified. Bore a hole through the length of the jam chuck to allow a wooden dowel to be used to push the work off should it become stuck.

With the pot held on the friction chuck, bring up the tailstock for support. Remove the bulk of the

Fig 19.6 *With the pot held securely on the jam chuck, an angled tool is used to undercut the base of the foot.*

waste from the underside of the foot using small cuts from a ¼in (6mm) spindle gouge. If the force on the work is too excessive, the work may spin on the friction chuck leaving a burn mark on the surface. The base should be turned to leave a concave face. Because the tailstock is supporting the work, a small area in the centre will not be accessible; this will need to be finished off by hand later. The appearance of the underside can be improved further if the base is turned with a definite step at the edge. To create this hollow step, use the tip of a small, angled hollowing tool (see Fig 19.6). Once the foot has been completed the stem details can be turned. Start at the bottom of the pedestal and work in stages towards the underside of the bowl. Sand and polish the stem before removing the pot from the lathe. The small pip left in the centre can now be removed, using the tip of a sharp gouge, and then sanded by hand.

To reverse the lid of the pot I prefer to use a four-jaw chuck, fitted with either wooden or nylon jaws, as the work is too thin to risk holding in a jam chuck. Alternatively, a wooden collet chuck can be made by making eight saw cuts in a cylinder and hollowing out the centre (see Fig 19.7). Turn a small step in the end to provide a location for the lid and use a jubilee clip to lightly clamp the lid in place. The decorative details can then be turned into the underside of the lid, using a small spindle gouge (see Fig 19.8).

Fig 19.7 *A home-made collet chuck can be used if the work is of a fragile nature. Note the hole in the side of the chuck to aid removal of the work.*

Fig 19.8 *The decorative details are turned with a small spindle gouge.*

For the lids of hollow vessels, or other plug-type stoppers, a cup chuck can be turned (see Fig 19.9). The plug of the lid, or stopper, can then be held in the recess with a push fit while the top face is turned.

Reversing bowls

For regular bowls with turned rims the process is relatively straightforward. If a four-jaw chuck is available then a set of stepped wood jaws can be made and the bowl lightly clamped in these (see Fig 19.3). Alternatively, a jam chuck can be made. The most

efficient way of doing this is to use a part-turned bowl of a larger size than the bowl being reversed. Using a parting tool, turn a shoulder in the rim to suit the bowl (see Fig 19.10). If you place a cloth between the bowl and the jam chuck before you begin work, the bowl can be easily removed afterwards (see Fig 19.11). If this is not done, the bowl may be difficult to remove, especially if it is of thin section. With either method, jam chuck or wood jaws, it is advisable to use a low speed and bring up the tailstock for support. However, if you are using a swivel-head lathe with the

Fig 19.9 *For plug-type lids and stoppers, cup chucks can be used to hold the work. They can be improved further by changing the cup chuck into a simple collet chuck, as shown in Fig 19.7.*

Fig 19.10 *A shoulder can be cut in the rim of a large bowl and used as a friction chuck to reverse smaller bowls.*

Fig 19.11 *A cloth should be placed between the bowl and jam chuck to aid removal of the bowl and prevent damage to its rim.*

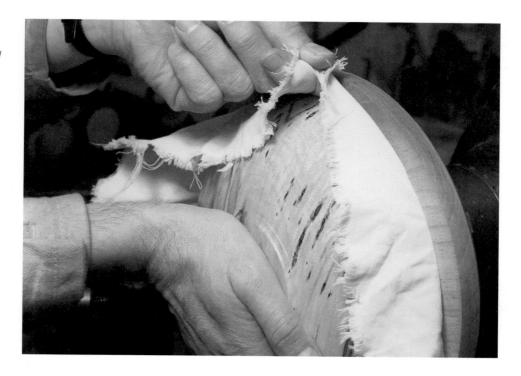

head at an angle to achieve the dimensional capacity required, this will not be possible. In these situations extra care must be taken and fine cuts used to prevent the work popping out of the jam chuck.

For reversing natural-edged bowls, I prefer to use a circular foam block held in the chuck. For the piece shown in Fig 19.12, I used the centre of a foam drum sander. A piece of cloth over the centre to prevent the retaining bolt from touching the inside of the

bowl may be necessary on shallower bowls. I pushed the bowl onto the foam, using the tailstock to apply the pressure. If you have left the original centre mark in the base of the work, you can use it to centre the bowl when reversing.

While there are other methods of reversing natural-edged bowls, I find this to be the best. The work does not slip, as the foam provides a positive grip inside the bowl, and yet does not leave any marks.

Fig 19.12 *A foam cylinder held in the chuck can be used to drive natural-edged bowls.*

Fig 19.13 *A spindle gouge is used to remove most of the waste from the foot of the bowl.*

The bulk of the waste can then be removed, using light cuts from a spindle gouge (see Fig 19.13), and the underside of the foot can be recessed using the tip of an angled hollowing tool in the same way as for turning the pedestal of a pot (see Fig 19.6). Once this is done, remove the bowl from the lathe and cut off the nib in the centre using the end of a sharp gouge (see Fig 19.14). To sand the inside of the foot, roll up a piece of abrasive and hold it in the chuck jaws. The end of the tube will then be able to reach into the corners of the recessed foot without rounding over the crisp edges (see Fig 19.15).

Reversing hollow vessels

When reversing a hollow vessel with a smooth-rimmed opening, I prefer to use a friction chuck method. As the openings to the majority of my vessels have a tapered mouth, a jam chuck with parallel sides is not suitable. Because of this, I turn a spigot chuck with a slight taper to match the angle of the opening in the vessel. This can often be turned into the waste wood left after parting off the work (see Fig 19.16). To prevent the work from being marked, cover the spigot with a piece of soft cloth before bringing up the tailstock for support.

For hollow vessels with a bark-edged mouth, I use a method similar to the one I use for natural-edged bowls, but instead of a dome-shaped block of foam, I use a piece with a conical recess in the middle.

Spouted vessels can be reversed on a small, parallel spigot chuck (see Fig 19.17), though because of the small area of contact, extra-fine cuts are necessary to prevent the work from slipping and leaving burn marks.

Fig 19.14 *The remaining pip can be cut away using a small carving gouge.*

Fig 19.15 *The hollow of the foot is sanded with a rolled-up tube of abrasive held in the chuck.*

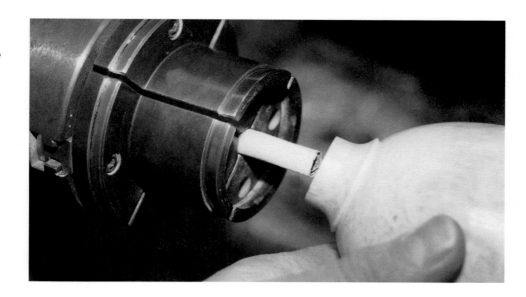

Fig 19.16 *A tapered friction chuck is turned into the waste wood after parting off.*

Fig 19.17 *Extra care must be taken not to let the work spin if the area of contact between the friction chuck and the work is small. If this is not done, the slipping will leave burn marks.*

looking AHEAD

HOPEFULLY, THROUGHOUT THE COURSE of this book you will have learnt a great deal. You will have built on your existing skills and learnt to apply them to a number of different applications. Now you have come to the end, but this does not mean you can just switch off the learning process until my next book comes along. Flick back through the pages of the Galleries. What catches your eye, and why? Maybe there are designs that could be merged to create new work (see Fig 20.1). Sometimes you will even find a piece of timber which already suggests a certain design (see Fig 20.2).

Inspiration

By now you will probably have seen many other examples of woodturning, including both contemporary and historical pieces. Look further still into other areas such as glass and ceramic work, even jewellery. Shapes that work well in one media will probably work well in another. Take a trip to museums to seek different shapes in materials other than wood. Make notes if necessary but do not sketch the work while you are there, make a sketch the following day.

Fig 20.1 *Oak burr. Diameter: 3¼in (83mm). I turned this square-edged bowl to provide a change from the flared, natural-edged bowls I normally make.*

Fig 20.2 *Wild cherry burr. Diameter: 9in (229mm). This bowl was made from a slab cut off the top of a burr. The figure and shape was so pleasing I felt that anything other than a near flat surface would spoil it.*

By then your mind will already have begun to mutate the image, and a new shape will have started to evolve. For each design that catches your eye, try to make three or four variations based around your memory of the original. By doing this you will soon be creating your own individual designs, and also developing an eye for good form.

As a creator of beautiful objects you should already be aware of your surroundings. The shape of a flower, the profile of a wooded horizon, the line of a river and so on. But what about less obvious profiles? The curve of an animal's tail, the arc of a bridge, anything. The list is endless. In time you will find yourself looking at everything in your field of view, constantly absorbing the shapes. It is this constant awareness that will allow you to gather a large mental gallery of different shapes that can be called upon to suit a particular piece of wood.

In the second and third galleries there are a few examples where the designs have been coloured, as in Fig 20.3. This has been done to enhance the figure and draw attention to it, not to try and improve on what nature has already created. Different combinations of colour are used to suggest different things, or feelings; stillness, movement, winter and so on. Many of the coloured designs I create are inspired by something I have seen, experienced or even heard. For similar reasons I add texture to some of my work, either with or without the addition of colour (see Fig 20.4). It is when you start to explore the use of surface treatment that you begin to realize the enormous potential that still lies ahead.

Fig 20.3 *Horse chestnut. Height: 12in (305mm). The surface of this vase has been coloured to change the effect. The result is a long way from the almost white colour of the natural wood.*

Fig 20.4 *Walnut (sapwood). Diameter: 11½in (292mm). Texturing a surface not only adds a point of focus, it also challenges our perception of a vessel.*

205

Metric Conversion Table

INCHES TO MILLIMETRES AND CENTIMETRES

in	mm	cm	in	cm	in	cm
1/8	3	0.3	9	22.9	30	76.2
1/4	6	0.6	10	25.4	31	78.7
3/8	10	1.0	11	27.9	32	81.3
1/2	13	1.3	12	30.5	33	83.8
5/8	16	1.6	13	33.0	34	86.4
3/4	19	1.9	14	35.6	35	88.9
7/8	22	2.2	15	38.1	36	91.4
1	25	2.5	16	40.6	37	94.0
1 1/4	32	3.2	17	43.2	38	96.5
1 1/2	38	3.8	18	45.7	39	99.1
1 3/4	44	4.4	19	48.3	40	101.6
2	51	5.1	20	50.8	41	104.1
2 1/2	64	6.4	21	53.3	42	106.7
3	76	7.6	22	55.9	43	109.2
3 1/2	89	8.9	23	58.4	44	111.8
4	102	10.2	24	61.0	45	114.3
4 1/2	114	11.4	25	63.5	46	116.8
5	127	12.7	26	66.0	47	119.4
6	152	15.2	27	68.6	48	121.9
7	178	17.8	28	71.1	49	124.5
8	203	20.3	29	73.7	50	127.0

Useful Addresses

When requesting information from any of the following, please help them by sending a large, self-addressed envelope.

Organizations: USA

AAW (Association of American Woodturners)
3200 Lexington Avenue
St. Paul, MN 55126

International Wood Collectors' Society
BILL COCKRELL (secretary)
2300 West Range Line Rd
Greencastle
IN 46135-7875
Organization for all those interested in collecting different timber species.

Organizations: UK

AWGB (Association of Woodturners of Great Britain)
LIONEL PRINGLE (secretary)
The Downs View
Hailsham Rd
Stone Cross
Pevensey
East Sussex BN24 5AS

Forestry Authority
231 Corstorphine Road
Edinburgh EH12 7AT

International Wood Collectors' Society
KEN SOUTHALL (secretary)
Aspen Cottage
Nettlestead
Ipswich
Suffolk IP8 4QT
Organization for all those interested in collecting different timber species.

NPTC (National Proficiency Testing Centre)
Avenue J
National Agricultural Centre
Stoneleigh
Warwickshire CV8 2LG
Listing of nationally approved chainsaw instruction courses.

Suppliers: USA

Craft Supplies USA
1287 E 1120 S
Provo
Utah 84606-9915
Axminster four-jaw chuck, BCWA drives, Chris Stott hollowing tools and general accessories. Catalogue available.

David Ellsworth
Fox Creek
1378 Cobbler Road
Quakertown, PA 18951
Hollowing tools (not available outside the USA).

Woodcraft Supply
PO Box 1686
Parkersburg, WV 26102-1686
Sorby multi-head revolving centre and general accessories. Catalogue available.

Suppliers: UK

Axminster Power Tools
Chard Street
Axminster
Devon EX13 5DZ
Four-jaw, self-centring chucks and general accessories. Catalogue available.

BCWA
93 Park Way
Coxheath, Maidstone
Kent ME17 4EX
Hollowing tools, bead-forming tools, mini drives and chuck accessories. Catalogue available.

Chris Stott
Croft House
Burringham
North Lincolnshire DN17 3NA
Miniature hollowing tools.

GB Servicing
Unit 23
Pier Road Industrial Estate
Gillingham
Kent ME7 1RZ
Movable stop switches and variable speed units.

Melvyn Firmager
Nut Tree Farm
Stoughton Cross
Wedmore
Somerset BS28 4QP
Hollowing tools and fine-bladed parting tools. Catalogue available.

P&J Dust Extraction
Extraction House
Otterham Quay
Rainham
Kent ME8 8NA
Adjustable extraction hood support and extractor units. Catalogue available.

Robert Sorby Tools
Athol Road
Sheffield S8 0PA
Multi-head revolving centre and general turning tools. Catalogue available.

Woodlots
Beacon Forestry
2A Rutland Square
Edinburgh EH1 2AS
UK-wide timber sales information.

About the Author

ROBERT CHAPMAN WAS BORN, and still lives, in Kent. His early experiences as a child, at school and on his father's lathe, planted the woodturning seeds. Always keen on woodwork he wanted to enter the industry upon leaving school but instead served a four-year engineering apprenticeship. So much for wanting to work in wood.

Robert took up woodturning seriously after the hurricane of 1987 hit south England; not wishing to see all the wood go to waste he bought a lathe. He is self taught but has learnt much from others, particularly through the formation of the AWGB.

Early on he made many of his own turning tools and work holding equipment. Word soon spread and other turners began asking him to make specialist tools for them. His tools and chuck accessories are now available commercially, marketed by BCWA.

With his work selling successfully, he left engineering to pursue woodturning as his full-time profession. His work is now sold through a number of galleries and craft exhibitions.

During his woodturning career he has been placed on the register of the Worshipful Company of Turners, selected for the Society of Designer Craftsman, and placed on the South East Arts selective index. He has also been awarded the certificate of excellence by the British Craft Guild and is the first woodturner outside the county to have been selected for the Sussex Guild of Craftsman.

Robert's work will already be familiar to many woodturners as he has written a number of articles for woodworking magazines.

As well as teaching woodturning, Robert has also demonstrated and lectured at various venues, including many AWGB groups and the Irish Woodturners' Guild seminar. He can also be seen exhibiting his work at some of the larger craft exhibitions within the UK.

Index of Timbers

A

acacia (robinia) *Robinia pseudoacacia* UK 22, 137
amboyna *Pterocarpus indicus* Papua New Guinea 12
ash
  Fraxinus excelsior UK 14, 16, 21, 23, 93, 151, 182, 186, 189, 190, 193, 194

B

beech *Fagus sylvatica* UK 12, 16, 17, 18, 30, 127, 130, 135, 166, 172, 175, 187, 188
birch *Betula pendula* UK 16, 180
blackboy (grass tree) *Xanthorrhoeaceae preissi* Australia 138, 183
bocote (Mexican rosewood) *Cordia gerascanthus* Mexico 12, 78, 81, 182
box *Buxus sempervirens* UK 12
buckeye *Aesculus* spp. USA 193

C

cherry *Prunus avium* UK 23, 137, 151, 191, 204
cocobolo *Dalbergia retusa* Mexico 12, 78, 81, 82, 83, 84

E

ebony *Diospyros* spp. 13
  African *Diospyros crassiflora* Africa 12, 77, 89, 187, 188
  Papua New Guinean (Asian) *Diospyros ferrea* Papua New Guinea 12, 77, 81, 83, 86, 90, 192
  Sri Lankan *Diospyros ebonum* Sri Lanka 166, 171
elm *Ulmus* spp. UK 13, 22, 30, 90, 134, 138, 184

eucalyptus *Eucalyptus* spp. Australia 12, 22, 23, 176, 177

G

gimlet *Eucalyptus salubris* Australia 12, 182
goncalo alves *Astronium fraxinifolium* Brazil 80
gutta percha *Excoccaria pervifolia* Australia 12

H

hairy oak (rose she oak) *Allocasuarina torulosa* Australia 12, 23
holly *Ilex aquifolium* UK 13, 177, 191, 193
hornbeam *Carpinus betulus* UK 30
horse chestnut *Aesculus hippocastanum* UK 181, 186, 188, 189, 190, 193, 205

J

jarrah *Eucalyptus marginata* Australia 132

K

kingwood *Dalbergia cearensis* Brazil 12, 63, 66, 79, 81, 83, 85, 87, 88, 89

L

laburnum *Laburnum vulgare* UK 13, 19, 22, 30, 94, 136, 194
lignum vitae *Guaiacum coulteri* Nicaragua 31, 78, 84
lilac *Syringa vulgaris* UK 19

M

madrona *Arbutus Menziesii* USA 12

mallee *Eucalyptus* spp. Australia 17
manzanita *Arctostraphylos* spp. USA 12
maple *Acer* spp. 14, 16, 98
  field *Acer campestre* UK 116, 138, 158, 181, 185, 188
  North American *Acer macrophylla* USA 141, 166, 171, 180, 192
  rock (including bird's-eye and quilted) *Acer saccharum* USA 129, 131
masur birch *Betula alba* Finland 12, 30, 84, 116, 135, 194
mulberry *Morus nigra* UK 93
musk *Olearia argophylla* Australia 12

O

oak *Quercus* spp. UK 13, 21, 30, 98, 129, 131, 133, 151, 189, 204
olive *Olea europaea* Spain 30
orange box *Celastrus dispermus* Australia 194
Osage orange *Maclura pomifera* USA 12, 67, 76, 81, 182
ovankol *Guibourtia ehie* Africa 90

P

padauk *Pterocarpus soyauxii* Africa 13
palm tree (coconut palm) *Cocus nucifera* Sri Lanka 12, 30
pau rosa *Swartzia madagascar* Africa 35, 45
pequia *Aspidosperma eberneum* Brazil 13
pernambuco *Caesalpinia echinata* Brazil 55

General Index

WOODCARVING

The Art of the Woodcarver	GMC Publications
Carving Birds & Beasts	GMC Publications
Carving on Turning	Chris Pye
Carving Realistic Birds	David Tippey
Decorative Woodcarving	Jeremy Williams
Essential Tips for Woodcarvers	GMC Publications
Essential Woodcarving Techniques	Dick Onians
Further Useful Tips for Woodcarvers	GMC Publications
Lettercarving in Wood: A Practical Course	Chris Pye
Power Tools for Woodcarving	David Tippey
Practical Tips for Turners & Carvers	GMC Publications
Relief Carving in Wood: A Practical Introduction	Chris Pye
Understanding Woodcarving	GMC Publications
Understanding Woodcarving in the Round	GMC Publications
Useful Techniques for Woodcarvers	GMC Publications
Wildfowl Carving – Volume 1	Jim Pearce
Wildfowl Carving – Volume 2	Jim Pearce
The Woodcarvers	GMC Publications
Woodcarving: A Complete Course	Ron Butterfield
Woodcarving: A Foundation Course	Zoë Gertner
Woodcarving for Beginners	GMC Publications
Woodcarving Tools & Equipment Test Reports	GMC Publications
Woodcarving Tools, Materials & Equipment	Chris Pye

WOODTURNING

Adventures in Woodturning	David Springett
Bert Marsh: Woodturner	Bert Marsh
Bill Jones' Notes from the Turning Shop	Bill Jones
Bill Jones' Further Notes from the Turning Shop	Bill Jones
Bowl Turning Techniques Masterclass	Tony Boase
Colouring Techniques for Woodturners	Jan Sanders
The Craftsman Woodturner	Peter Child
Decorative Techniques for Woodturners	Hilary Bowen
Faceplate Turning	GMC Publications
Fun at the Lathe	R.C. Bell
Further Useful Tips for Woodturners	GMC Publications
Illustrated Woodturning Techniques	John Hunnex
Intermediate Woodturning Projects	GMC Publications
Keith Rowley's Woodturning Projects	Keith Rowley
Multi-Centre Woodturning	Ray Hopper
Practical Tips for Turners & Carvers	GMC Publications
Spindle Turning	GMC Publications
Turning Green Wood	Michael O'Donnell
Turning Miniatures in Wood	John Sainsbury
Turning Pens and Pencils	Kip Christensen & Rex Burningham
Turning Wooden Toys	Terry Lawrence
Understanding Woodturning	Ann & Bob Phillips
Useful Techniques for Woodturners	GMC Publications
Useful Woodturning Projects	GMC Publications
Woodturning: Bowls, Platters, Hollow Forms, Vases, Vessels, Bottles, Flasks, Tankards, Plates	GMC Publications
Woodturning: A Foundation Course (New Edition)	Keith Rowley
Woodturning: A Fresh Approach	Robert Chapman
Woodturning: A Source Book of Shapes	John Hunnex
Woodturning Jewellery	Hilary Bowen
Woodturning Masterclass	Tony Boase
Woodturning Techniques	GMC Publications
Woodturning Tools & Equipment Test Reports	GMC Publications
Woodturning Wizardry	David Springett

WOODWORKING

Bird Boxes and Feeders for the Garden	Dave Mackenzie
Complete Woodfinishing	Ian Hosker
David Charlesworth's Furniture-Making Techniques	David Charlesworth
Furniture & Cabinetmaking Projects	GMC Publications
Furniture Projects	Rod Wales
Furniture Restoration (Practical Crafts)	Kevin Jan Bonner
Furniture Restoration and Repair for Beginners	Kevin Jan Bonner
Furniture Restoration Workshop	Kevin Jan Bonner
Green Woodwork	Mike Abbott
Making & Modifying Woodworking Tools	Jim Kingshott
Making Chairs and Tables	GMC Publications
Making Fine Furniture	Tom Darby
Making Little Boxes from Wood	John Bennett
Making Shaker Furniture	Barry Jackson
Making Woodwork Aids and Devices	Robert Wearing
Minidrill: Fifteen Projects	John Everett
Pine Furniture Projects for the Home	Dave Mackenzie
Router Magic: Jigs, Fixtures and Tricks to Unleash your Router's Full Potential	Bill Hylton
Routing for Beginners	Anthony Bailey
The Scrollsaw: Twenty Projects	John Everett
Sharpening Pocket Reference Book	Jim Kingshott
Sharpening: The Complete Guide	Jim Kingshott
Space-Saving Furniture Projects	Dave Mackenzie
Stickmaking: A Complete Course	Andrew Jones & Clive George
Stickmaking Handbook	Andrew Jones & Clive George
Test Reports: The Router and Furniture & Cabinetmaking	GMC Publications
Veneering: A Complete Course	Ian Hosker
Woodfinishing Handbook (Practical Crafts)	Ian Hosker
Woodworking with the Router: Professional Router Techniques any Woodworker can Use	Bill Hylton & Fred Matlack
The Workshop	Jim Kingshott

UPHOLSTERY

Seat Weaving (Practical Crafts)	Ricky Holdstock
The Upholsterer's Pocket Reference Book	David James
Upholstery: A Complete Course (Revised Edition)	David James
Upholstery Restoration	David James
Upholstery Techniques & Projects	David James

TOYMAKING

Designing & Making Wooden Toys	Terry Kelly
Fun to Make Wooden Toys & Games	Jeff & Jennie Loader
Making Wooden Toys & Games	Jeff & Jennie Loader
Restoring Rocking Horses	Clive Green & Anthony Dew
Scrollsaw Toy Projects	Ivor Carlyle
Scrollsaw Toys for All Ages	Ivor Carlyle
Wooden Toy Projects	GMC Publications

DOLLS' HOUSES AND MINIATURES

CRAFTS

GARDENING

VIDEOS

MAGAZINES

WOODTURNING ✦ WOODCARVING ✦ FURNITURE & CABINETMAKING
THE DOLLS' HOUSE MAGAZINE ✦ CREATIVE CRAFTS FOR THE HOME
THE ROUTER ✦ THE SCROLLSAW ✦ BUSINESSMATTER ✦ WATER GARDENING

The above represents a full list of all titles currently published or scheduled to be published.
All are available direct from the Publishers or through bookshops, newsagents and specialist retailers.
To place an order, or to obtain a complete catalogue, contact:

GMC Publications,
Castle Place, 166 High Street, Lewes, East Sussex BN7 1XU, United Kingdom
Tel: 01273 488005 Fax: 01273 478606

Orders by credit card are accepted